365

smart

After-school activities

TV-Free Fun Anytime for Kids Ages 7–12

Sheila Ellison and Dr. Judith Gray

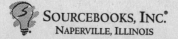

SOURCEBOOKS, INC.®
NAPERVILLE, ILLINOIS

Published by Sourcebooks, Inc.
P.O. Box 4410, Naperville, Illinois 60567-4410
(630) 961-3900
FAX: (630) 961-2168
www.sourcebooks.com

Previous edition cataloged as follows:
Ellison, Sheila.
     365 afterschool activities : TV-free fun for kids ages 7-12 / by Sheila Ellison and Judith Gray.
          p. cm.
    ISBN 1-57071-080-5 (pbk.) : $12.95
     1. Creative activities and seat work. 2. Amusements. 3. Handicraft. I. Gray, Judith Anne.
II. Title.
  GV1201.E58   1995
   790.1'91 — dc20
95-23996

                                        CIP

Printed and bound in the United States of America.
BA 10 9 8 7 6 5 4 3 2

Acknowledgments

I want to extend a sincere thank you to Gabrielle Crescini for her time spent testing activities with my children and others, and for the many invaluable hours she has spent providing person support to me and my children. And a special thanks to Bryan Hidalgo, for his friendship, enthusiastic support of this project, proofreading, editing, and legal advice.

—Sheila Ellison

Dedications

To my daughters Wesley and Brooke, for coming home each day after school with new ideas for me to write, for their wonderful drawings, and for keeping their brothers entertained while I finished, "Just one more activity!"

—Sheila Ellison

To Jonathan and Andrew,
For the most wonderful boys you have been and the successful men you became.

—Judith Gray

Introduction

This book is for parents, teachers, youth leaders, and families. But most of all, it is for kids who want fun and imaginative activities to enjoy after school and during weekends—activities which also have easy-to-find materials and clear directions.

Older kids like lots of action with built-in challenges and creativity. *365 Smart Afterschool Activities: TV-Free Fun Anytime for Kids Ages 7–12* is designed to meet the needs of children who have time and energy on their hands—and what kids don't!

Our book has something for every kid, from games and puzzles to music and crafts. There are ideas for room decorating, field trips, parties, reading, writing, and community involvement. The activities are safe, constructive, and age-appropriate. It is our hope that parents and other adults will join their children in the adventures within these covers.

We welcome and appreciate your comments and suggestions. Please write to us at Sourcebooks.

Contents

Friendship

Games

Hobbies

Horticulture

Music

Nature

Number Magic

Parties

Puzzles

Reading Activities

Repairs

Room Decoration

Science

Self-Esteem

Teach Yourself

Textiles

Visual Arts

Writing

Businesses for Kids

Bedding Plants

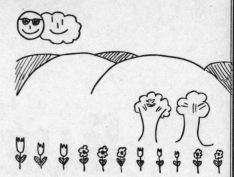

Materials
Potting soil mix
Milk cartons
Used pony packs or small containers
Plastic wrap
Assorted seeds—parsley, tomatoes, cabbage, chives, marigolds, zinnias, asters, sunflowers, squash, poppies

Directions
During the winter, buy seeds to start inside. With scissors, cut off one side of a milk carton and staple the opening. Fill halfway with potting soil and lightly sprinkle with water to dampen. Sow seeds, one kind per carton, according to the directions on the packet. Label the carton or staple the seed packet to one end. Cover with plastic wrap and place in a dark, dry place until seeds germinate. Remove wrap and place in a sunny spot, watering often. When seedlings are 2 or 3 inches high, transplant 6-8 into smaller plastic containers. In a few weeks they will be ready for sale.

Let your neighbors know that you have bedding plants for sale and watch them disappear!

Note: Find a good gardening book and check for climate and soil suitability when selecting seeds.

1

Cards and Letterheads

Materials
Computer and printer
Good quality paper and matching envelopes
Word processing or desktop publishing software

Directions
If you have computer skills, you can produce personalized letterheads and matching envelopes for friends and family members. Your only costs are the paper and toner. You can also produce flyers, announcements, brochures, greeting cards, invitations, and forms. As your business increases, design yourself an order form complete with your name, logo, address, phone number, and price list. The quality of your order form will bring business your way.

Note: Color printing is more expensive and so is color copying. However, there may be special orders which will require you to use color...charge a little more.

Gift Wrapping

Materials
Assorted rolls of wrapping paper
Colored ribbons and matching bows
Clear adhesive tape
Empty gift boxes
Tissue paper (sheets)
Gift tags
Scissors

Directions
Before you begin wrapping gifts for other people, practice gift wrapping with newspaper and items around the house, such as books, socks, toys, and boxes of different shapes. Now neatly wrap a box or book in wrapping paper complete with ribbon, bow, and gift tag. You can use this sample to show your potential customers. Start offering your services to neighbors and busy working moms and dads. Allow your customers to choose the paper and the gift tag. Make sure you have all your materials with you and that you schedule enough time to complete the job to everyone's satisfaction.

Note: Some stores may let you set up a table at holiday time for a few hours per day. Show the store manager your sample and the gift wraps you plan to use when making your request.

Childcare

Materials
Story books
365 Days of Creative Play
Healthy snacks
365 Games Smart Babies Play

Directions
For this idea, it is best to be at least 10 years old and to know how to take care of small children. Aside from evening babysitting, you should consider watching children after school until parents get off work, playing with children on Saturdays or Sundays, doing childcare during school holidays when parents are working, and staying with children before school when parents have to leave early to go to work. Also consider asking the managers of hair salons, athletic clubs, tanning booths, nail care salons, and health clubs if they could use childcare services. Adult parties and gatherings usually need a babysitting service, especially for baby and wedding showers, Tupperware parties, support groups, volunteer meetings, and women's clubs. Check your local newspaper for dates and times of meetings, then call and see if they need a sitter.

Note: If you are hired to babysit for a meeting, arrive 10 minutes early to meet the children and their parents. Plan games, puzzles, and quiet activities. Bring lots of books. When the meeting is over, tidy the room

Pet Care

and get the children ready to leave.

Directions

Pet-sitting services are always in demand, particularly during vacation time. You can care for large animals in their own homes, dropping by each day to feed, water, and exercise them. Smaller animals such as hamsters, mice, birds, and lizards can stay in their cages and be kept in your own home. Small fish tanks can be moved to your home, but large ones will need daily attention. Obtain written, detailed care instructions from the owners and also get the phone number of a veterinarian. Advertise your services at pet stores, supermarkets, and veterinarian offices.

Note: You can also consider breeding and selling small animals such as hamsters, mice, gerbils, and rabbits.

Lemonade Stand

Materials
Fresh lemons
Sugar
Water and ice
Large pitcher
Paper cups
Small table and
Tablecloth
Signs

Directions
Prepare the lemonade the night before, using fresh lemon juice, sugar, and hot water. If lemons are too expensive, use frozen concentrate. Refill the ice cube trays several times and store the ice cubes in a large plastic bag in the freezer. Make large colorful signs to advertise your business and consider offering two sizes—large and small cups. On the day of the sale, place your lemonade stand in a good location where a lot of people will notice it. Take along a cooler for the ice and a money box with some change in it.

Note: Look for weekend neighborhood garage sales or events at a nearby park. Choose a warm, sunny day and erect a sun umbrella to draw more attention to your business.

Tie-Dye T-Shirts

Materials
Fabric dyes in assorted colors
Large plastic tubs
Wooden spoons
Plain white T-shirts in
several sizes
Strong rubber bands

Directions
Mix the dyes according to the directions on the packets. Use a separate tub for each color and stir with a wooden spoon. Tie knots in the T-shirt or twist sections and secure with rubber bands. Dip the tied T-shirt into a dye tub and swirl around until covered. Leave for the time indicated on the dye packet. Remove and rinse with water until the water runs clear. Allow to dry. Untie the knots and remove the rubber bands. Iron flat or tumble in a clothes dryer to remove creases. Experiment with more than one color and with imaginative tying designs.

Tutoring Math and Reading

Materials
Dictionary
Calculator
Note paper
Pens and pencils

Directions
If you have a fairly good grade point average and get along well with your peers and younger children, you are a good candidate for a tutoring business. Most parents are anxious to have their children succeed at math and reading.

Offer to travel to the home of the person needing tutoring and take along your materials. Consider designing a flyer to advertise your tutoring business and distribute it in elementary schools and youth organizations. Make sure you are available after school and weekends.

Note: A special and rewarding challenge is tutoring students with learning disabilities. See your Special Needs teacher at school and ask for advice and strategies. You could also volunteer to help out during school hours and develop some skills in this area.

Lawns and Yardwork

Materials
Small garden tools
Rake
Large bags for clippings
Yard broom
Trimmer or shears
Garden gloves
Lawn mower (optional)

Directions
First practice your lawn mowing and garden care skills on your own back-yard. Know how to use and maintain garden tools and equipment. Ask a parent to evaluate your work and follow any suggestions for improvement. Advertise your services by placing a flyer on your neighborhood front porches. You can mow lawns, weed, trim edges, rake leaves, dig holes for planting shrubs, water gardens, lawns, and planters, remove caterpillars and snails, clean and weed driveways, plant bulbs, pick fruit and berries, and turn compost heaps. Be sure to clean up afterward by sweeping walks and driveways and bagging clippings, weeds, leaves, and trash.

Note: To be really successful, arrange to mow lawns or maintain gardens on a regular weekly basis. Keep a schedule of your clients' names, addresses, and their yardwork needs. Be prompt, prepared, and professional.

Pet Grooming

Materials
Pet shampoo
Flea and tick shampoos
Bath brush
Towels
Hair brushes and combs
Hair dryer
Large tub

Directions
Dog and cat grooming is a good business if you like animals and you don't mind getting wet. First, make sure you have a secure area where dogs can be washed and rinsed. Remove burrs or knots before wetting. Follow the directions on the shampoo bottle and avoid getting shampoo in the animal's eyes, ears, and mouth. After rinsing thoroughly, pat with a towel and allow the dog to shake. Small dogs can be dried with a hair dryer on low temperature. Using a wide-toothed comb, comb the hair starting low and working towards the backbone. Finally, brush the coat in the direction of the natural fur lines.

Note: Cats and other small animals should not be wet-shampooed. Combing and brushing are acceptable and there are insecticidal powders for the removal of fleas and ticks. Carefully follow the directions.

10

Car Washing and Detailing

Materials
Plastic bucket
Detergent
Wool mitt or soft sponge
Chamois cloth (optional)
Towels
Window cleaner
Soft cloths
Vacuum cleaner
Vinyl cleaner (optional)
Toothbrushes

Directions
Close all windows and doors after making sure the hand brake is on. Rinse exterior of car with water and remove caked mud and dirt with a soft brush. Follow directions on car soap container or pour a few drops of detergent onto damp mitt or sponge. Soap and rinse the car a section at a time, starting with the rooftop and ending with the tires. Towel dry and then buff with chamois. Vacuum the inside floor coverings and seats. Wipe the vinyl with cleaner or a damp cloth. Clean windows, dials, and mirrors. Use toothbrushes to clean small, narrow spaces. Use a dry cloth to shine the chrome. Charge extra for waxing and polishing.

Note: At family functions or parties at your home, ask if you can wash cars while the owners are visiting. Have plenty of supplies on hand, especially towels and cloths.

Snow or Leaf Removal

Materials
Snow shovel
Whisk broom
Leaf rake
Yard broom
Large bags

Directions
A snow-shoveling service is in great demand in those areas of the country where winter snowfalls are the rule rather than the exception. Be available to clear driveways, sidewalks, and steps immediately after it has stopped snowing. On most days, this will mean doing the work before school. For a steady income, arrange a winter-long contract with neighbors.

Leaf raking can be done after school and during weekends. Be prepared with a rake, broom, and bags. Know exactly where the bagged leaves are to be left or stored and make sure you do a thorough job. For a steady income, also arrange for a fall contract.

Note: If you are reliable, punctual, polite and do a good job, word-of-mouth will result in more jobs.

Window Cleaning

Materials
Glass cleaner (or vinegar
and water)
Paper towels or dry cloths
Small, portable stepladder
Soft brush

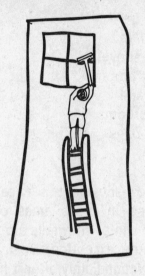

Directions
Offering your services as a window cleaner
will bring you plenty of customers. You
should offer to clean windows both on the
inside and the outside. Before you begin,
remove any mud, spider webs, or dirt film with a soft brush or rag.
Spray on the glass cleaner and wipe off while still wet, remembering to
get into the corners. Using a clean, dry cloth or paper towel, polish thoroughly one more time. Change towels frequently and repeat the process
if the window is still not sparkling clean. Avoid getting the glass cleaner on any finished wood surfaces. Dispose of the used paper towels or
take home the cloths to be washed, dried, and used again.

Note: Leave an announcement or flyer describing your window cleaning
service at the houses in your neighborhood. Include the times you are
available and the amount(s) you charge.

Aide to Elderly

Directions

Many elderly people would appreciate help with household chores and errands. Here are some services that you could offer: taking out the garbage, housecleaning, exercising the dog, going to the Post Office, sweeping driveways and paths, opening mail and reading it out loud, weeding, returning books to the library, making telephone calls, preparing snacks or meals, loading

and emptying the dishwasher, washing laundry, making beds, cleaning windows, and accompanying them on walks. To find elderly people who may need your help, contact retirement homes, community services, and elderly day care centers.

Note: Check with your own grandparents about jobs and errands they would most like help with. Offer your services free to them in return for a letter of reference.

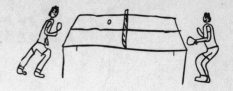

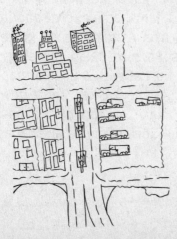

Community
Involvement

Holiday Baskets

Materials
Basket
Ribbon
Liner or cloth napkin
Assorted holiday foods
Assorted small, useful gifts

Directions
Before you start, contact your local Social Services agency for families, elderly folk, and handicapped people who would like to receive a holiday basket. Knowing who is going to receive your basket will help you decide on the contents. Next, purchase or make the holiday foods— breads, fresh fruit, canned food, dried food, jams, coffee, etc., and items that individuals, such as children, would like. Also purchase groceries such as toothpaste, soap, hand lotion, soup mix, salad dressing, tea bags, sugar, and other staples. Drape the basket with a liner or napkin. Arrange the holiday and staple items inside the basket. Tie a bow on the handle and write a holiday note to place on top of the basket. Deliver the basket to the recipient or to the Social Service agency a few days before the holiday.

Special Olympics

Directions

Special Olympics is an international organization which provides year-round training and athletic competition for mentally retarded individuals aged 8 years and over. There are many opportunities for volunteering your time and assistance, especially at the sports events. For example, at volleyball tournaments, youth volunteers are needed to time, score, chase stray balls, run results, and hand out awards. Older kids can help anytime after school in the office doing filing, phone calls, bulk mailing, and data entry. At any Special Olympics event, you can cheer on the athletes and show your support.

Note: Write to:
Special Olympics International
1133 19th St., NW
Washington, DC 20036
www.specialolympics.org

Special thanks to Karen Chemotsky of Everett Parks and Recreation Department who is the Area Director of Special Olympics.

Adopt-a-Block

Materials
Plastic bags
Rubber gloves

Directions
Choose a block in your town or city. The best choice will be the one that you live on. Make a brochure to let the residents or your neighbors know that you are getting involved in your community and would like to help keep the block clean and tidy. Include your name and phone number and the days and times that you will be cleaning up. You can also list the things that people can do to help. On clean-up day, put on rubber gloves and pick up litter for 1-2 hours. You can also keep a written tally of how many items you picked up and what kind. This would be helpful information to share in your next Adopt-a-Block brochure.

Note: Mail your brochure to city hall.

Girls and Boys Clubs

Directions

Go to www.bgca.org to find a club near you. If there are no Boys or Girls clubs, the local YMCA would also be a good option. Call and ask for the Executive Director or the Director of Programs. Explain that you are interested in volunteering and outline the days and hours you can work. Fortunately, these youth clubs operate after school, early evenings, and sometimes during the weekends. You may be invited to assist with the programs or to help around the facility. In either case, your involvement will be highly appreciated and you will enjoy working with younger kids and your peers.

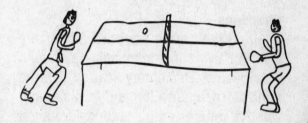

Note: Boys and Girls Clubs and Girls, Inc. are national youth organizations committed to the education, well-being, and positive growth of young boys and girls. Girls, Inc., founded as Girls Clubs of America in 1945, is an expanding national network of over 200 centers located in more than 120 cities devoted to serving girls' special needs.

Tutoring

Directions

Volunteer tutoring opportunities are plentiful in your community. Start with your nearest elementary school. Call the principal or counselor and explain that you are interested in tutoring younger students. You can give your strengths—reading, math, sports, drawing, library research, geography, etc.—and also the hours you would be available. You will be most effective if you can tutor on a regular basis and with the same student. You can also offer to tutor children in their homes, especially with homework. Students can also be dropped off at your home in the early evenings or weekends, provided you have a quiet place to study together.

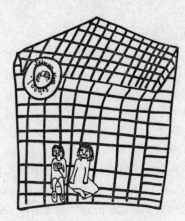

Note: A very rewarding tutoring situation is to help newcomers to America speak and read English. Contact the ESL teacher at your school or at the nearest community college for this volunteering opportunity.

Toys for Tots

Directions

Since 1947, the Marine Corps Reserve has sponsored toy collections and giveaways to disadvantaged children in most cities across the country. You and your friends can donate new, unwrapped toys, especially around holiday time. You can also volunteer to help or send a donation. Call your local chapter of the Toys for Tots Foundation to find out where you can drop off your toys and how you can get involved.

Adopt-a-Family

Directions

At any time during the year, you and your family can offer to adopt a low-income or homeless family. This involves purchasing groceries, providing birthday and holiday gifts, contributing toys,

clothing, toiletries, household items and blankets, and purchasing movie and bus passes. Your generosity will be greatly appreciated and family members will feel more connected to the community that surrounds them.

Note: Visit your library or call the Salvation Army, Big Brothers and Big Sisters, American Red Cross, Jewish Family Services, Catholic Family Services, and YMCA or YWCA.

21

Food Bank Volunteer

Directions

Call your local food bank (ask at your library for the phone number and address) and ask about volunteering opportunities. Jobs you can do will involve sorting foodstuffs,

stacking shelves, and filling food boxes for families. You may also want to organize a mini food drive in your neighborhood so that you can bring food contributions to the food bank where you are volunteering.

There are also opportunities during times of national or world disasters where gathering food, blankets, or donations would be of great help. Listen for breaking news and meet the needs where you see them.

Graffiti Removal

Materials
Paintbrushes
Paint rollers and tray
Paint

Directions
Graffiti in our neighborhoods is unsightly and is a form of vandalism. There are ways you can help prevent and remove graffiti from walls and fences. You should always report new graffiti to a law enforcement agency whether it is on private property or not. An officer of the Youth Gang Unit will want to take a look before it is removed. If the graffiti is on private property, you will need permission of the owners to paint over it and they will want to make sure you have the right color paint. city hall will want to take care of the graffiti removal if it is on city property, but you can always offer to help. To prevent graffiti, arrange for a police officer to visit your school and talk to the students about the causes, effects, and consequences of graffiti.

Senior Center Helper

Directions

Most communities have senior centers where older citizens congregate, participate in organized activities, and enjoy each other's company. A Center Director usually plans the activities and supervises them. There are many opportunities for volunteering after school and during the weekends. Senior centers need young people to help with activities and events such as bazaars, evening meals, holiday celebrations, classes, outings, and flea markets. They often need help with setting up, serving, and cleaning up. Also, if you are good at crafts or gardening, a senior center would be a great place to offer your services. Contact the director of your local senior center and get involved!

Adopt-a-Pet from the Humane Society

Directions

It is not necessary to buy expensive pets from a pet store or breeder. The Humane Society in your town or county has many homeless animals that would make wonderful pets. Visit the nearest animal shelter over a period of a few weeks to see which animals are  available to adopt. There will be cats, dogs, birds, rats, hamsters, gerbils, and others. The pets stay at the shelter as long as they are healthy and there is room for them. When you have made your selection you will have to fill out an application form (to show the Humane Society that your pet is going to a good home) and pay a fee. Buy a pet care book or borrow one from the library on how to take good care of your newly adopted pet.

Note: Humane centers also need pet caretakers. Many offer training programs in pet care for their volunteers.

25

Cooking

Fruit Salad

Ingredients
Any kind of fruit you like
Lemon juice

Directions
Wash and cut the fruit into chunks and gently mix them in a bowl. Squeeze half a lemon or one tablespoon lemon juice over

the fruit and stir. A few ideas of what to do with fruit salad: put it on top of ice cream, put it in crepes or pancakes, make Jell-O and spoon some in. You can add many things to your fruit for variations. Try adding whipped cream, sour cream, mayonnaise, yogurt, celery, chopped carrots, nuts, or raisins. Be creative and see what you can come up with!

Note: For a fancy fruit dessert, buy a pound cake and instant vanilla pudding. Cut the pound cake into squares, prepare the pudding according to the directions, then layer the cake, pudding, and fruit.

Fruit Freeze

Ingredients
Real fruit juice
Paper cups
Fruit, cut in pieces (optional)

Directions
Pour fruit juice into paper cups, add fruit if desired. Place in freezer until frozen solid. To eat, rip back paper at top of cup while holding fruit freeze at the bottom. By the time you get to the bottom, it should be slushy enough to drink.

Note: Put fruit juice into ice cube trays to use as decorative additions to lemonade or other light colored drinks.

Pancakes

Ingredients

2 eggs
3 tablespoons melted butter
2 cups milk
2 cups flour
2 teaspoons baking powder

Directions

With a wire whisk, mix together the eggs, butter, and milk. Add the flour and baking powder and stir with the wire whisk until lumps are gone. Put one tablespoon vegetable oil in a frying pan over medium-high heat. With tea cup or soup dipper, pour batter into pan making three-inch circles. Watch pancakes. When little bubbles can be seen all over, turn them over. When both sides are brown, they are done. Things you might want to serve with pancakes: maple syrup, jam, powdered sugar and lemon, sliced bananas, strawberries, blueberries, yogurt, whipped cream, or ice cream.

Note: When you get good at making pancakes, plan a pancake breakfast for your friends or family, with the proceeds going to a local shelter.

Egg Variations

Ingredients
Eggs
Milk
Butter

Directions
Omelet: Put two eggs in a mixing bowl with one tablespoon milk. Beat with a fork. Put one table-spoon butter in frying pan over medium-high heat and pour in eggs. Using a pancake turner, push the eggs around in the pan until they begin to get lumpy, then take them off the heat. Flatten them to the thickness of a picture book. Sprinkle anything you want on top: cheese, onions, sliced tomatoes, etc. Turn heat to low and put a lid on, placing frying pan back on the stove. Let cook 3 to 5 minutes, then flip one half of the omelet over the other half. Put on a plate and eat.

Scrambled eggs: Do the same as for omelet, but continue to push the eggs around the pan until completely cooked.

Fried eggs: Put one tablespoon butter in a frying pan over medium heat. Crack the egg on the side of the frying pan. Open shell with thumbs placed in the crack and pull shell apart so egg falls into pan. Cook for 3 minutes, then flip over on other side and cook for 2 minutes more.

Soda Fizz

Ingredients
4 quarts water
3 tablespoons ginger
½ lime
2 ½ cups sugar or honey
3 tablespoons cream of tartar
1 tablespoon yeast
Cheesecloth or coffee filter
Funnel
Gallon jug with cap or cork
Large pot with lid

Directions
Boil the water in the pot. Add ginger, juice from lime, sugar, and cream of tartar and mix well. Let the mixture cool to lukewarm (not too hot or cold. If the water is too hot it kills the yeast). Add yeast and mix well. Cover pot and let the mixture set for six hours. Now bottle your soda. Strain it through the cheesecloth or coffee filter that sets into the top of a funnel. Leave an air space at the top of the bottle. Once the soda is in the bottle, cap it tightly and put it into the refrigerator. Wait two days, then slowly unscrew the top of the jug. Cheers!

Popcorn

Ingredients
⅓ cup vegetable oil
⅔ cup popping corn
3 quart saucepan with lid
Optional: Butter, raisins, peanuts,
peanut butter, honey, grated cheese,
onion, or garlic salt

Directions
Put oil in saucepan over high heat and add popcorn. After the first kernel pops, put the lid on and begin moving the saucepan back and forth over the element. If pan gets too full, you may need to empty some of the popped corn into a bowl. When all the corn is popped, add what you like to it. Here are a few ideas:

- Melted butter and salt
- Mix one cup peanut butter and half cup honey in a bowl. Heat in a microwave for 2 minutes. Then pour over popcorn and mix.
- Press the peanut popcorn into oiled pan and cut into squares.
- Melt cheese in the microwave and pour it over the top.

Note: Popcorn pops because of the explosion of the molecules of water inside the kernel.

Chocolate Chip Cookies

Ingredients
1 cup butter
¾ cup brown sugar
¾ cup white sugar
1 egg
1 teaspoon vanilla
2 cups unbleached flour
½ teaspoon baking soda
1 cup chocolate or carob chips

Directions
Preheat oven to 350°F (180°C). Cream butter, sugars, egg, and vanilla until fluffy. Mix in flour, salt, and baking soda. Add chocolate chips. Drop by tablespoons onto a greased cookie sheet. Bake for 12 to 15 minutes. Yield: 24 cookies.

Note: These cookies are flat and chewy. For a thicker, fluffier cookie add ¼ cup flour.

Quesadillas

Ingredients
3 six-inch (150mm) flour tortillas
Vegetable cooking oil or butter
1 cup shredded white cheese
1 cup shredded yellow cheese
½ cup finely chopped tomato
Parsley or cilantro leaves

Directions
Lightly fry each tortilla in one tablespoon oil or butter until crisp and golden, turning once. Sprinkle with combined cheeses and top with tomato. Put lid on pan and turn heat to low. When cheese is melted, fold tortilla in half. Cut each tortilla into quarters. Garnish with parsley or cilantro leaves. Serve warm. Yield: 3 servings.

Note: If using a conventional oven, place tortillas on a cookie sheet and bake at 350°F (180°C) for 10 minutes, or until cheese is melted.

Granola

Ingredients
4 cups uncooked oats
½ cup coconut
½ cup almonds or seeds
½ cup bran or grapenuts
¼ cup butter or margarine
¼ cup honey
½ cup raisins or dates

Directions
Mix first four ingredients. Melt butter and honey and stir into dry ingredients. Spread evenly on cookie tray. Bake at 300°F (150°C), stirring often, for 20 minutes. When finished cooking, stir in raisins. Cool before storing in airtight jar or container. Yield: 12 servings.

Shakes

Ingredients

Milkshake:
2 cups low-fat milk
3 scoops vanilla ice cream
2 teaspoons natural jam, carob
Powder or chocolate sauce

Yogurt shake:
1 cup nonfat fruit flavored yogurt
1 cup favorite fruit juice
1 cup ice cubes

Directions
Put milkshake or yogurt shake ingredients into a blender and blend on medium-high speed for 2 to 3 minutes until smooth.

Party Sandwiches

Ingredients
¼ cup butter
⅛ teaspoon salt
1 tablespoon lemon juice
3 ounces (85g) cream cheese
5 thin slices of natural white bread
10 thin slices whole grain bread
20 thin tomato slices
20 thin cucumber slices

Directions
Mix together butter, lemon juice, salt, and cream cheese.
Using a round cookie cutter, cut 20 circles from the white bread and 40
circles from the whole wheat bread. Using the same cutter, cut one circle from each tomato and cucumber slice. Spread a half teaspoon
cheese mixture on one side of each bread circle. To assemble, layer
grain bread circle, tomato, white bread circle, cucumber, and grain circle. Put a toothpick through the sandwich and serve. Yield: 6 to 8 servings.

Pizza Map

Ingredients

Pizza crust:
¼ ounce package dry yeast
1 ⅓ cups warm water
2 tablespoons oil
1 teaspoon salt, 4 cups flour,
1 tablespoon sugar or honey

Pizza topping: 8 ounces pizza or tomato sauce, half pound grated mozzarella cheese, sliced vegetables, sliced sausage or pepperoni, any other desired toppings

Directions

First make crust. In a mixing bowl, dissolve the yeast in warm water, add oil and honey. Mix well and let stand for 5 minutes. Add flour one cup at a time and mix until dough is elastic, but not sticky. Put dough on a floured board and fold and press the dough for a few minutes. Take a teaspoon of vegetable oil and rub it around the inside of a bowl. Place the dough in bowl and cover with a towel. Let rise for 1 to 1½ hours or until doubled in size. Put dough on greased cookie sheet and shape the dough to look like a favorite country. Cover with tomato sauce and other toppings. Use the toppings to mark lakes, mountain ranges, rivers, state capitals or favorite vacation spots. Bake for 20 to 30 minutes at 375°F (190°C). The pizza is done when the cheese melts and the crust is brown.

Salad

Ingredients

Vegetables: tomatoes, radishes, celery, carrots, broccoli, cucumbers, mushrooms, lettuce
Cheese
Tea towel, sharp knife, cutting board, vegetable peeler

Directions

There are three important skills for you to know in making a salad:

1. **Peeling:** This is done with a vegetable peeler which scraps against the vegetable and removes skin. Vegetables to peel are carrots, cucumbers, zucchini, and potatoes.
2. **Grating:** This is done by rubbing the vegetable against the grater from top to bottom in one direction, making long thin strips.
3. **Slicing:** This is done using a serrated knife by holding the vegetable firmly on a chopping board with one hand while slicing with the other.

If you have never tried slicing, peeling, or grating, ask an adult to show you and then watch you to see if you are doing it right. Make sure to wash all the vegetables first and only peel the ones that need peeling. Rinse the lettuce leaves and wrap them in a clean tea towel, then swing them around your head so the water flies off the leaves into the towel. Serve your salad with pride!

Note: Make your own salad bar by leaving all the vegetables in separate bowls. Add bowls of raisins, nuts, and seeds.

Vegetable Dip

Ingredients
Peeled and cleaned vegetables

Cheese dip:
4 tablespoons cream cheese soft-
ened in the microwave for 15 seconds, 2 tablespoons sour cream or
plain yogurt, 1 teaspoon chopped
chives, salt and pepper

Pink dip:
4 tablespoons mayonnaise, 2 tablespoons tomato ketchup

Directions
Pick which dip you would like to make and put the ingredients in a
bowl. Mix them with a fork. Serve with assorted vegetables (see activity 38 for instructions on peeling and slicing vegetables).

39

Vegetable Stir-Fry

Ingredients
Butter or vegetable oil
Vegetables
Salt and pepper

Directions
See activity 38 for instructions on slicing, peeling, and grating vegetables. For stir-fry, the vegetables need to be cut in small bite-size pieces.

Put three tablespoons butter or vegetable oil in a frying pan. Turn the heat on medium-high (if you don't know how, ask an adult). When the butter has melted, add the vegetables and stir them around for about 5 minutes. Shake a little salt and pepper on top like you were salting food on your plate. Stir frequently. Then add four tablespoons water and cover with a lid. Turn the heat down to low. The vegetables will be ready to eat in 5 minutes.

Note: These cooked vegetables can be added to many things such as omelets, pasta, or quiche. To make a soup, pour a can of chicken or beef broth (instead of water) over vegetables and let simmer 5 minutes.

Baked Potatoes

Ingredients
Potatoes
Toppings:
Cheese
Sour cream or
plain yogurt
Chives
Bacon bits

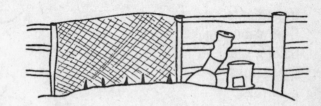

Directions
Scrub your potatoes very well, then use a fork to prick each potato several times. Put a paper towel in the microwave oven. Arrange the potatoes evenly on top of the paper towel. Microwave on high power for 12 to 14 minutes. Take them out using an oven mitt and let stand for 5 minutes. Cut them in half and sprinkle with toppings of your choice. You could also make stuffed potatoes by cutting them lengthwise, then scooping the centers out into a mixing bowl. Mash the potatoes with a fork and add a bit of sour cream or yogurt, butter, and salt. Beat with an electric mixer until smooth. Spoon back into the potato skins. Top with cheese and bacon and microwave for one minute, or until cheese is melted.

Roast Chicken and Vegetables

Ingredients
One whole chicken
Baking dish
4 potatoes
4 carrots
1 cup chicken broth
Salt and pepper
Olive oil

Directions
Preheat oven to 350°F (180°C). Before you start, a word of caution—
when dealing with raw chicken, wash your hands immediately after
touching it and wash off all utensils and cutting board before slicing
vegetables. Peel and slice potatoes and carrots (see activity 38). Take
whatever is inside of the chicken out and throw it away. Put chicken in
casserole dish and surround it with carrots and potatoes. Rub olive oil
over the top of the chicken, then sprinkle with salt and pepper. Pour
broth around edges. Bake for 1 1/2 hours. Cut chicken off bones (you
may need help for this) and put on plate with potatoes and carrots.

Correspondence

Thank-You Letters for Gifts

T
H
A
N
K
▯
Y
O
U

Thank-you   THANK-you

THANK-you
Thank-you

ꊽ ᴐ⅃ ⊓ ₊ tnant

Materials
Writing paper or card
Pen
Envelope
Postage stamp

Directions
The letters that kids write most frequently are thank-you notes. It is important to thank friends and family members for gifts and other kindnesses you have received. When writing a thank-you note for a gift, be sure to mention what the gift was and how you were able to enjoy it. Thank-you notes are written on a card or small sheet of paper with matching envelope. The date and address are typically placed in the lower left-hand corner under your signature. An example follows:

Dear Aunt Penny,
Thank-you for the book, *Black Beauty.* I have always loved stories about horses and one day hope to have a horse of my own. Thank you for remembering my 12th birthday.
    Love,
    Elizabeth

Note: Thank-you notes should be sent no later than one week after you receive the gift.

43

Writing to the President

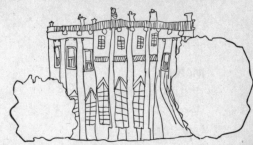

Materials
Writing paper
Pen
Envelope
Postage stamp

Directions
There are many reasons kids would like to write to the president. They might be concerned about the environment or youth crime. Your letter will be read by a White House secretary who may refer it to the president. No matter who reads it, however, you will receive a reply.

Your letter can be neatly handwritten or typed. It should be short and to the point, with your concern clearly stated. Here is an example:

Dear Mr. President,
I am a 6th grader at Jackson Middle School and I am very concerned about the depletion of the ozone layer. I don't want to grow up in a world that is unprotected from the harmful effects of direct sunlight. I am writing this letter to ask you to help by increasing penalties for companies with harmful environmental practices. Please do whatever you can.

Note: The address for the president is:
The President of the United States
White House Office
1600 Pennsylvania Avenue NW
Washington, DC 20500

Party Invitations

Materials
Writing paper or cards
Pen
Envelopes
Postage stamps

Directions
After your parents have given you permission to have a party, you need to prepare a list of friends you would like to invite. Send out party invitations no later than one week before the party. The invitations can be bought or you can design your own. In either case, each invitation must include the following:

- The date and time of the party
- The address of the party
- Your full name
- Reason for the party or a brief description if it is a special event
- RSVP and your phone number

Note: RSVP is a French abbreviation—*répondez s'il vous plaît*—which means, "please reply."

Letters of Complaint

Materials
Writing paper
Pen
Envelope
Postage stamp

Directions
A letter of complaint is a form of business letter. It is better to type this kind of letter because it will be easier to read and you can make a copy for your own records.
Place your full address and the date in the upper right-hand corner. Write the name and address of the person or company to whom you are complaining on the left-hand side. Start with "Dear Sir or Madam" if you do not have the name of the person. In the first paragraph, clearly outline your complaint with brief details. Next, describe how you would like to be compensated. Finally, in your third paragraph, thank the person for reading your letter and say that you are looking forward to having the matter promptly resolved. Conclude with "Sincerely Yours" and your signature underneath.

Note: To really get results, send a copy of your letter to your local Better Business Bureau.

46

Letter Endings

Directions

By the time you get to the end of a letter, it is often hard to think of something interesting to say. Those last few lines of your letter are the lines that will be remembered. Write something positive and cheerful and beware of words or sentences that may unintentionally hurt feelings. Sometimes it is hard to think of a way to say goodbye. Most often, you will simply write "With Love" or "Much Love," especially if it is to a family member or close friend. Other friendly endings are "Fondly," "Warmly," "Best Wishes," "Warm Wishes" and "Affectionately." Formal letters end with "Sincerely" or "Sincerely Yours."

Note: P.S. at the end of a letter (after the signature) means "postscript." It is used when adding a message or extra information.

Secret Letter Codes

Materials

Writing paper
Pen
Envelope

Directions

A secret code letter is exchanged between best friends only. You and your friend need to put your heads together and create a secret code that no one else can decipher or understand. One way is to use the letters of the alphabet in a different sequence, e.g., A=B, B=C, C=D, etc., so that DOG would = EPH. Or you could use symbols, pictures, or a rebus, e.g., 2 Y's U R, 2 Y's U B, I C U R 2 Y's 4 me (too wise you are, too wise you be, I see you are too wise for me). A secret code letter does not usually need an envelope. It can be folded neatly and passed by hand to your friend. And if someone else opens it, he or she will never know what's inside!

Note: Do not pass secret code notes in class. Teachers are known for their ability to decode any student note that they find in their classrooms.

Rhyming Letters

Materials
Writing paper
Pen
Envelope

Directions
Rhyming letters are fun to receive and even more fun to write. First, you might want to make lists of rhyming words. Check with a dictionary to make sure they are spelled correctly. Now you are ready to begin. For your first attempt, make every second line rhyme. Here is an example:

> I wish you were here
> To be with me today.
> We could trade baseball cards
> And then go out to play.

With practice, you could rhyme every line. Illustrate your rhyming letter or draw an interesting border around it. Your family and friends will be most impressed.

Note: If you have a special poem that you like, you could copy it instead of creating your own and send it as a letter. Remember to include the name of the poet.

Writing Fan Letters

Materials
Writing paper
Pen
Envelope
Postage stamp

Directions
If you have a favorite sports star, movie star, or singer, there is no reason why you cannot write a letter to that person. You can even request an autographed photo. It is generally not possible to mail a letter directly to a famous person. However, you can contact his or her fan club or the appropriate sports franchise and your letter will be forwarded. Fan letters should start with a brief description of yourself and where you go to school. The middle of the letter should describe an occasion (game, film, or concert) when you saw the famous person perform. End your letter with a request for a photo and a reply. Make sure you include your complete mailing address.

50

Wax Seals for Important Letters

Materials
Colored sealing wax
Brass stamp
Candle
Candleholder

Directions
After you have written or typed (word processed) your letter, fold it neatly and place in an addressed envelope. Apply a postage stamp and place your name and address in the top left-hand corner of the envelope. Seal the envelope and turn it face down on a clean surface. Light the candle and place in a candleholder. Carefully melt the sealing wax in the candle flame, being careful not to drip the wax onto your skin. Let the sealing wax drop onto the back side of the envelope on top of the flap point. When there is a mound of soft wax the size of a quarter, gently press the stamp on top and hold until the wax is hard.

51

Apology Letter

Materials
Writing paper
Pen
Envelope
Postage stamp

Directions
We all make mistakes and poor decisions. Every once in a while our mistake makes it necessary to write an apology letter. (We can also apologize face-to-face or over the telephone.) A letter of apology has four parts or sentences:

1. Say you are sorry for the mistake you made.
2. Explain what you could have done differently so that the mistake would not have occurred.
3. Offer some restitution—a way to "mend" the situation.
4. Promise that you will not make the same mistake again.

Here is an example:

Dear Mrs. Jones,

I am sorry that my baseball knocked over and broke your potted plant. I should have practiced my throwing in the park. I don' t know how much a new pot will cost, but I would like to buy you another one. I promise I will be more careful in the future.

> *Sincerely,*
> *David Meyers*

Thank-You for Overnight Stay

Materials
Writing paper
Pen
Envelope
Postage stamp

Directions
After visiting with a friend overnight, it is necessary to write a thank-you letter to your friend's mother or father. This letter should be written neatly and sent within 3 days after you get home. Recall a special event or kindness that occurred during your stay and mention it in your letter. Here is an example:

Dear Mrs. McLaughlin,
Thank-you so much for a great weekend in your home. It was fun to spend time with Julie and Brian and to play in your newly landscaped yard. I especially enjoyed the day at Great America. Brian and I must have tried every single ride!
My mother sends her best wishes. Thank you again for everything.
*   Warmly,*
*   Jonathan*

Note: These letters are often called "bread and butter" letters.

Friends Overseas

Materials
Writing paper (or aerogram)
Pen
Envelope
Overseas postage
Internet connection

Directions
Keeping in contact with someone your age who lives in another country is a very exciting thing to do. There are many organizations online. One that connects students in many countries is www.world-pen-pals.com. All it takes is some of your time and a slightly more expensive postage stamp or quick email. Using an aerogram is a very convenient alternative. Friends overseas mostly want to hear about you, your family, your school, and the things you like to do. They will also like to receive photos of you, your family, and your pets. Find out the birthday of your overseas friend and surprise her or him with a birthday card!

Note: Start a stamp collection with the stamps from your overseas mail. Also, when applying your stamps, see how many different ones you can place on the envelope. That way, your overseas friend can start a stamp collection too.

Crafts

Masked Container

Materials

Interestingly shaped bottle or jar
Masking tape
Shoe polish (brown or tan)
Scissors, rubber gloves, soft cloth

Directions

Wash the bottle inside and out and let it dry thoroughly. Tear or cut pieces of masking tape and apply them to the bottle, working from the bottom to the top. As each piece is placed, be sure it is flat and that it overlaps another piece. Continue until the entire bottle is covered with tape pieces. Wearing rubber gloves, coat the tape pieces with a thin layer of shoe polish. Once dry, use a soft cloth to buff the coating of shoe polish. The finish will look antique.

Jigsaw Puzzle

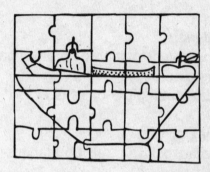

Materials
Piece of cardboard
Colorful picture or art supplies
to paint your own
Glue, scissors
Clear acrylic

Directions
Choose a colorful picture you like from a calendar, a magazine, or a poster. Draw your own if you like. Glue the picture onto the cardboard. When it is dry, cover the picture with clear acrylic as a protective coating. When the coating is dry, cut the cardboard into small pieces with scissors. The more pieces you make, the harder it will be to put it together, so think of the age of the person who will be "puzzling."

Note: Try writing a letter, making a puzzle out of it, then putting it in an envelope to send to a friend or relative!

Paper Beads

Materials
Paper—construction paper, wallpaper, or magazine pages
Round toothpicks or nails
Glue
String or yarn
Shellac, paint, or felt tip markers

Directions
Begin by cutting the paper into straight and triangular strips. The width, length, and shape of the strip determine the size and shape of the bead. Experiment and see what shapes you like. Cover one side of the paper strip with glue, then place the toothpick or nail at one end. Use a toothpick if you want to put the bead on string, use a nail if you want to string the bead on yarn. Roll tightly into a compact bead. Remove the toothpick or nail before the bead dries. Let the bead dry thoroughly before adding coloring and shellac (shellac darkens the color of the bead). String the beads in a design you like.

Note: These make nice gifts and would be a fun project at a party.

Wrapping Paper

Materials
Paper to print
Poster paints
Styrofoam shapes
Sponge
Textured wallpaper
Candle wax
Colored ink

Directions
There are three different kinds of paper designs to try in this activity.
- The first is with the paint and Styrofoam or sponge. Cut the Styrofoam or sponge into desired shapes. Put paint in a shallow pan and dip the shape into the paint, then make five or six marks on the paper. It is fun to do the "stamping" in a row because the paint thickness will vary and it will look interesting. Experiment with design and color.
- Now try an ink wash effect. Dampen the paper with a cotton ball soaked in water. When the paper is still wet, drop colored inks onto the surface and allow the colors to mix. Tilting the paper makes the colors run together for a different effect.
- The next wrapping paper is a textured rubbing. Place paper over a textured surface like old wallpaper, wood grain, stone, or cement. Rub candle wax over the paper. Soak ink or paint into a cotton ball and spread it evenly over the surface of the paper. Watch how the textured surface pattern suddenly appears.

Sliding Puppet Stage

Materials
Poster board (cardstock)
Double-sided tape or glue
Poster paints
Large box for stage

Directions
Create your own fairy tale theater. Decide what story you want to tell—either your own or an old favorite. Draw the characters yourself or trace them from a book. Color them and cut them out. Glue or tape them onto a one-inch by twenty-inch piece of cardstock (the strip of cardstock needs to be as long as the box opening). The strip of cardstock will move the character from side to side within the stage. Cut out some other pieces of scenery and paint the inside of the box as a backdrop. You may want to make a curtain out of cloth. Cut slits in one side of the box and insert character strips. Write the script and put the puppet show on! Once the box is constructed, make new characters and backdrops when you want to change the show.

Play Dough

Materials
4 cups flour
1 cup iodized salt
1 ¾ cups warm water
Food coloring or paint powder

Directions
Mix the above ingredients together in a large bowl and knead for 10 minutes. If you want to make hard-baked figures, just bake at 300°F (150°C) until the dough is hard. You can also air dry the dough for a few days and it will become hard. Paint and varnish the figures if you like. Store dough in plastic wrap or airtight container.

Monster Mask

Materials

Cardboard box that will fit over your head

Paint

Cotton balls, tissue paper, wrapping paper, foil, bubble wrap, and other decorations

Glue, scissors

Directions

Paint the outside of the cardboard box. Now the fun starts as you create the monster's features. Paint on a scary face, glue things to the top and sides. Painted bubble wrap makes good hair. Foil can be shaped into horns, whiskers, ears, or anything else you can think of. When you have finished your creation, put it on your head and have someone help you mark the eyes. Cut holes so you can see out. Put the mask on and "become" the monster. If you want to make a body to go with the mask, get a large cardboard box and paint it. Then cut holes for the head and arms.

Recycled Bowl

Materials
3 or 4 paper egg cartons
Wallpaper paste
Plastic cling wrap
Small bowl
Paints and brushes

Directions
This is an easy way to make a bowl that looks like pottery. Start by taking the egg cartons and ripping them up into small pieces. Put the pieces in a pot and cover them with boiling water. Every day for a week, mush up the egg cartons. When the pieces are really soft, squeeze out the water. Mix up some wallpaper paste according to directions on the package and add the glue slowly to the paper making a sort of paper clay. Cover the inside of the bowl with plastic cling wrap. Gently press the paper clay to the sides of the bowl. Try to make the covering as thin as possible. Leave it to dry on a warm windowsill. When it is dry, take it out of the bowl by pulling on the plastic film. If it is still a little wet, put it in a warm oven until dried. Paint it when dry, and after the paint dries, coat it with clear varnish. This bowl cannot hold liquids.

Plastic Bracelet and Necklace

Materials
Clear plastic tubing ¼ inch and
½ inch (get at a hardware store)
Felt tip pens, scissors, craft knife,
cutting board
Modeling material (Fimo, Formellos, Prima)
Foil, baking sheet, Kleenex
Thin knitting needle

Directions
Shape your hand as if you were going to slide a bracelet on your wrists.
Wrap the tubing around your knuckles and mark where the ends meet.
Roll the modeling material into a snake, thin enough to fit into the tube,
about three inches long. Bend the modeling material to form the same
curve as the bracelet tube when the ends are held together. Bake the
modeling material in a 250°F (130°C) oven for 20 minutes, then allow it
to cool. In the meantime, roll up the Kleenex and cut it into 20 pieces,
then color the pieces with felt tip pen (you could also use rice paper or
wrapping paper). Roll the paper into small pieces and stuff into the tube
using the knitting needle. Work from both ends until the tube is nearly
full. Leave a half inch at each end. Do the necklace the same as the
bracelet. Cut two one-inch pieces from the cooled modeling material to
stuff into the ends of the tube to close. Experiment by putting other
things into the tube like metal balls, beads, seeds, or powder paint.

Shrunken Apple Head

Materials
Large red apple
Piece of string
Large darning needle
Button
Vegetable peeler

Directions
Thread the piece of string through the needle, tie the end to a button, then poke the needle through the core of the apple starting at the bottom moving up toward the stem. Peel the skin off your apple, then carve the apple into the shape of the head you want to make. Make indentations for the eyes and mouth and carve some of the apple away around the nose to make it stick out. Take the apple and place it in the sun to dry out. Don't put it outside or the birds will eat it! A window ledge that gets sun would be perfect. Within days it will start to shrink. In the first few days, you can still make cuts in it to encourage the shape you want. When it is dry, push dried cloves in it for eyes. You can paint the face or make a puppet out of it if you like.

Picture Mosaic

Materials
Colored paper
Black paper
Glue, scissors

Directions
Cut the colored paper into small squares no larger than one inch by one inch. Glue the squares onto the black paper creating a pattern or picture. Try to cover the entire black paper with tiny squares. Imagine what it was like to do an entire floor!

Note: Many floors in old churches had mosaic patterns made of cut glass and stone.

Paper Dolls

Materials
Cardboard
Paper
Scissors
Felt tips or crayons

Directions
Draw your own paper dolls or copy figures from a book onto the cardboard. Cut them out. Make each doll stand by cutting a half inch slit in the bottom of the doll, then put a half-inch by two-inch piece of cardboard strip through it. Make clothes for your doll. Look in fashion magazines to get ideas or make them up from your imagination. Make sure to cut tabs around the clothes so you can stick them on.

Soap on a Rope

Materials
Slivers of soap you have saved
Double boiler
Juice can or muffin tin for mold
Heavy yarn or twine

Directions
For this project, you need to save bits and pieces of soap—the more colors the better. Once you have many bits of soap saved, put them in the top part of a double boiler and fill the bottom part two-thirds  full with water. Bring the water to a boil, then reduce heat to a simmer. Stir the soap until it is melted. Ask an adult to help you with the stove and hot soap. When the soap is melted, pour it into the juice can or muffin tin "mold." Make sure someone helps you pour the hot soap. As the soap cools and hardens, insert two ends of folded 22 inch yarn or twine into the soap leaving the loop end out. When the soap is hard, remove from the mold by using warm water.

Papier Mache

Materials
Newspaper
Wallpaper paste
Balloon, large bottle, or
cake tin
Masking tape
Paint and brushes

Directions
Papier mache is made by building up layers of paper and paste over some sort of mold. When the paste dries, the paper will be firm enough to be painted and varnished. First, cover the mold with oil or Vaseline so you can pull the papier mache object off easily when it is finished. You will need to layer at least six pieces of glued paper to make a firm shape. To layer, tear paper into long strips and spread paste on each strip as you work. Repeat this until you have four layers, then paste these over your mold.

Let the papier mache dry thoroughly for two to three days before taking it off the mold. Glue overlapping strips of paper around the edges or trim edges with scissors. You can add handles or shapes to the basic mold by taping strips of card to it, then papier mache over the top. Paint when completely dry, then varnish.

Gak Attack

Materials
1 ½ cup white glue
1 cup water
¼ cup powder borax
Food coloring
Large bowl

Directions
Mix the glue and water together in the large bowl. Add food coloring. In a small cup, combine the borax and one tablespoon water. Mix. Pour the borax and water into the glue mixture and stir. A small lump will form. Take the lump out and squeeze it until it becomes non-sticky. Repeat the borax and water step until all the glue mixture has become gak. This recipe will make four to five balls.

Dance and Movement

Bunny Jump

Materials
Walking-pace music with a good beat

Directions
This dance can be performed alone with hands on hips, or with one or more friends, hands on the waist of the person in front. Start with feet together. Step left foot to the side and bring it back in (2 counts) and repeat. Step right foot to the side and bring it back in (2 counts) and repeat. Jump with both feet together to the front (2 counts), jump back (2 counts) then take 3 jumps to the front (1 count each). Rest for 1 count and start the dance over again. Altogether the dance is 16 counts. Practice a few times and then teach it to someone else.

Headstands

Materials
Flat pillow

Directions
It is important to practice headstands in a safe place and against a wall. Place the pillow on the floor for your head. Form a triangle with your forehead on the pillow and hands under your shoulders on the floor. Tuck your knees, slowly push off both feet and try to balance. Straighten your legs when you feel steady. Use the wall to maintain your balance. Later, when you are good at it, you can do a headstand anywhere without needing a wall.

Note: When you are an expert at headstands, experiment with ways to position your legs—out wide, toes pointed, one knee bent, splits.

Arms 2-3

Directions

This activity requires lots of concentration. Take your right arm and move it up above your head and down to your side, counting "one, two" each time. Repeat. Rest. Take your left arm and move it up above your head, out to the side at shoulder height and down to your side, counting "one, two, three" each time. Rest. Repeat. Now try to do both arms at once! Hint: Start with both arms moving up above your head. How long can you keep going?

Note: This is an excellent coordination exercise.

Cartwheels

Directions

First, you need to feel like a cartwheel looks. Stand in the shape of a star with arms outstretched and legs wide apart. Turn your body to the side, rock backwards a little and then, placing one hand on the ground after the other, move your body and legs like a wheel turning. At the start, your legs will be bent and your cartwheel will look like a bunny jump sideways. But don't give up! Gradually try to straighten your legs and evenly distribute your weight onto your hands and feet. Don't be afraid to ask someone to show you.

Note: Try to watch the Olympic Women's Gymnastics on tape or TV to see the world's best cartwheels performed.

Fabric Tubes

Materials
2 yards (meters) of stretch
kit fabric (tubular is best)

Directions
Measure the fabric so that it is wide
enough and long enough to cover
you from head to toe with your arms
outstretched. Stitch (or have an
adult stitch) the fabric into a tube with one end open. Turn right side
out. Slip the fabric tube over yourself and sit back and have others
watch the show! Here are some movements that work well for a "tube"
dance: stretching, rolling, poking, twisting, bending, reaching, bouncing,
jumping, pointing, and kicking. Since you will not be able to see what
your dance looks like, a friend or parent could get inside the tube and
dance too!

Note: Tube dancing makes a very entertaining group dance. Make some
extra tubes and invite friends over to join the fun.

Streamer Dance

Materials
Colorful wide ribbons or crepe paper streamers

Directions
Cut the ribbons or streamers into 6 foot (2 meter) lengths. Start with one ribbon and explore the many ways that the ribbon can make designs in the air. While standing

in one spot, try circles and loops above the head and close to the floor. Do up and down movements. Make a figure eight, small and then large. Make big and small circles out to the side with arm outstretched. Now try all these movements with 2 ribbons, one in each hand. Finally, move from place to place taking the ribbons with you. Try skipping, running, and walking. Perhaps you can find some music that blends well with your "streamer dance." Otherwise, you can sing or hum to accompany yourself.

Opposites

Directions

One way to explore creative movement is to use "opposites." Start on the floor, very relaxed and comfortable. Describe these words in movement:

> tense and relax
> wiggle and stiffen
> rock and roll
> curl and uncurl

Now stand up and express these opposites:

> stretch and squeeze
> rise and sink
> bend and straighten
> grow and wither

Try these words moving from place to place:

> walk and run
> march and meander
> crawl and slither
> tiptoe and leap
> fast and slow

Note: This activity can also help you with your vocabulary, especially antonyms.

Space Traveling

Directions

You are to imagine that you are in a space-craft that has been traveling through space for a long time. You have been asleep all the while. Now it is time to wake up and prepare to land. Sit on the floor in any comfortable position. Close your eyes and start to move your head—any way at all. Rest. Try moving your shoulders, one at a time and both together. Rest. Now move your elbows in all kinds of ways—add the wrists and fingers moving through the space around them. Add the moving shoulders and, finally, add the moving head. Add the movements of the back so that you are now moving the whole upper body. Rest. You can lie down on your back and explore the movements of the hips, knees, ankles, and toes, individually and together. When you are done, you will be ready to explore space!

Cultural Dance: The Hora

Directions

The hora is a dance that is usually performed in a circle with any number of dancers. The hora step can be performed individually or with a partner. Here it is:

Step to the left with the left foot (count 1)

Step with the right foot to the left, crossing in front of the left foot (count 2)

Jump on both feet, with feet close together (count 3)

Hop on left foot, while right foot swings slightly forward (count 4)

In place, take 3 quick steps—right, left, right—and hold (count 5 and 6)

Repeat step over and over again, going a little bit faster each time.

Note: The Hora is the national dance of Israel. It came from Romania.

Newspaper Dance

Materials
2 or 3 sheets of newspaper

Directions
There are many ways to create dances with a double sheet of newspaper. Open the newspaper and spread it on the floor. Skip around it; jump on it; run and leap over it; slither under it; swivel on it with your feet together. Now pick up the newspaper and wave it from side to side; run with it high in

the air; throw it up in the air and watch it float to the floor; repeat and then try to imitate the movement pattern of the newspaper. Next, crumple the newspaper into a ball; throw the ball and catch it; roll it along the floor and follow on your hands and knees; stand up and dribble it with your feet; lie on your back and hold the ball between your feet—how many different movements can you make? Finally, spread the paper out flat again; pick it up, and as you move from place to place, shred the paper into little pieces and toss them into the air like confetti; scoop up handfuls and throw into the air as you conclude the "newspaper dance."

Note: Be sure to pick up all the pieces of newspaper and take them to the recycling bin!

Basic Locomotor Steps

Directions

To perform any dance well, it is important to know the basic loco-motor steps. This activity will review the steps, practice them and try variations and creative possibilities.

Walk—forward, backward, sideways, on your toes, on your heels, with a turn

Run—lightly, smoothly, slowly, with small steps, sideways, lifting knees, prancing

Skip—softly, high, small steps, long steps, in place, backward

Leap—run and leap, leap high, with arms up, point toes, make a shape in the air

Hop—in place, forward, backward, changing feet, sideways, with a turn

Slide—change direction, 4 to the left and 4 to the right, point toes, low, high

Gallop—high, fast, slow, changing direction, changing feet

Jump—feet together, feet apart, in place, forward, sideways, knees bent, low

Note: Dance sequences can be created by combining these steps, e.g., run, run, leap, run, run, leap, step, hop, step, hop, jump, jump, jump, hold. Repeat.

Elastic Shapes

Materials
A continuous circular elastic band

Directions
To make the elastic band, measure yourself from head to toe and double it. Cut this length from a half-inch or three-fourths-inch (1-2 centimeters) elastic and securely knot the two ends together. Now you are ready to begin.

Explore shapes with the elastic while you are standing, sitting, lying, kneeling, and moving around the room. Also try using one arm and one leg, two legs and an elbow, your head and feet. Stretch the elastic tight or make it loose; twist and turn; bend and straighten; make fast movements and slow, gradual movements. Ask a friend to join you and create some interesting duets with one elastic band or two.

Note: Elastic can be purchased from department stores, fabric stores, and from tailors or seamstresses.

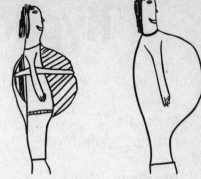

Drama

Hypnotized Play

Materials
Scarf or small towel

Directions
One person gets to be the magic wizard while the others sit as if they were asleep in their chairs. The wizard touches someone with the magic scarf and tells them  what they are to become. The person immediately becomes that person or thing. The wizard then touches the next person. Each person does their acting and when the wizard says "back to sleep," they move back to their chairs. It is also fun to suggest actions you do as yourself, like getting ready for school, talking with your brother, or baking a cake. Everyone gets a chance to be the wizard.

Laughing Hands

Directions

This activity involves two people. One person stands or sits directly in front of the other with hands behind the back. It is important that this person's arms do not show. The front person provides the voices and facial expressions for the scene. The person in back extends his or her arms around the front person and is the "hands." Pick scenes to act out that would involve hand movements such as putting something together, eating at a restaurant, brushing teeth, and washing your face. This is fun to do in front of an audience, so get family members or neighbors to watch. Let each person have a chance to be the "hands."

83

Shadow Play

Materials
Thick tape or thumb tacks
White sheet
Portable light
Dark room

Directions
Hang up the sheet in a way that doesn't damage the wall or ceiling. Put the light behind the sheet. Turn off the lights and act out a play between the sheet and the light. Get a few family members or friends to be the audience and see if they can guess what play you are acting out. The audience might want to try acting as well!

Note: On a warm summer night, try hanging a sheet across the garage door (with the door open). The entire garage can be used as the stage.

Silly Sentence Skit

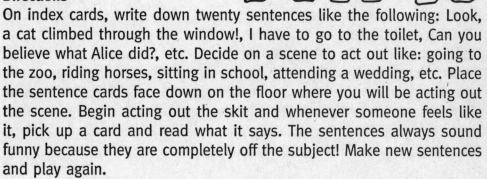

Materials
Index cards
Pen or pencil

Directions
On index cards, write down twenty sentences like the following: Look, a cat climbed through the window!, I have to go to the toilet, Can you believe what Alice did?, etc. Decide on a scene to act out like: going to the zoo, riding horses, sitting in school, attending a wedding, etc. Place the sentence cards face down on the floor where you will be acting out the scene. Begin acting out the skit and whenever someone feels like it, pick up a card and read what it says. The sentences always sound funny because they are completely off the subject! Make new sentences and play again.

Note: This is a fun game to play when sitting around with friends trying to decide what to do.

Bag Skit

Materials
Large paper bags
Various household items for props

Directions
This is a fun group activity, but can also be done alone and then performed for the family. Ask someone who is not playing with you to put twelve props into the large paper bag. Things like a dust pan, scissors, underwear, wig, rag, card, toy, or anything else they can find. Each group of two or more is given a paper bag and they must make up a skit using all the props in the bag. Have fun, laugh, and over exaggerate!

Television Act

Directions

Practice acting out favorite television shows, commercials, sporting events, news shows, game shows, or anything else you might see on television. Practice a little bit of each act. The audience members get to change the channel periodically. When this happens, actors must immediately change the theme to one of those practiced above. If more than one person is acting, let one person be in charge of whispering what is going to be acted out next, or write out the order so all the actors can see what to act when the channel is changed.

87

Change Your Shape

Materials
Old stretchy tights
Soft rags
String
Scissors

Directions
Characters come in all shapes and sizes! Here is how to exaggerate different body parts in order to better reflect the character being acted out. Cut one leg off the tights so you have a long tube. To make breasts, stuff the rags into the tube in two lumps and divide them with strings, tie the strings in between and on either side of the breasts. To make a bottom, do the same thing but stuff the lumps fuller. Make a fat, saggy person by filling two tubes with one big shape then strap one to your stomach and tie the bottom bulge to the waist strap and let it hang. To make a pregnant woman, use one large shape in the front. Once your shapes are in place, put clothes on top. Try to make other shapes for various characters.

Masks

Materials
Mask—made or bought

Directions
By changing your body movements, voice and actions, it is possible to become a different person or creature behind a mask. The idea is to put your mask on and see the world through the eyes of the mask char-

acter. The change of character must take place the moment the mask is put on and stop when the mask is removed. This is best done with two or more people so you can each act as your mask character to each other, but it can also be done alone using imaginary situations or a mirror.

Walk Your Character

Directions
Have you ever noticed the different ways people walk? Here are some walks to practice and get good at so you can use them in your acting.

- Limp on one leg, walking as if it hurts. You might want to put something in your shoe to help you remember which leg is supposed to be hurt.
- Strut by walking quickly with your head up and hands held behind your back, lean back a little, and take big steps.
- Hunch your shoulders, put your hands in your pockets, take small steps, and shuffle your feet.
- Wear high-heeled shoes, take small steps, bend your knees, and bounce as you walk.
- Toes both in or toes both out. Think about what characters would use which walk.
- Watch people next time you are out and try imitating them.

Imagination Stretchers

Directions
Closing your eyes and imagining some-thing in your mind gives you a chance to feel something, see something, be someone, or do something you are not actually doing. To try this, close your eyes and imagine yourself as some character from a story or play. Imagine your-self in a situation, see yourself acting it out, feel how you would feel as that person. Do this as many times as you like. This is great to do before you really act out a part to get into your character.

Mime

Directions

Mime is a form of acting which uses gestures and actions instead of words. You might have seen a mime on a street corner or on television. They usually have white faces and dress in black and white. The idea is to pick something you have done before and act it out using only gestures and actions: going to school, eating lunch, a birthday party, getting ready for school, talking on the telephone. Use your hands like you would normally; for instance, if you are opening a present, hold the present, put it next to your ear and shake, open the card, untie the ribbon, then open it. If you are walking around a room, make sure you walk around imaginary furniture, not through it. Use your facial expressions and remember, no sound! See if anyone can guess what you are doing.

92

Stage Movement

Directions

Actors don't usually stand in one place, they move around objects and other actors, use their arms, heads and bodies as they talk. A fun way to practice talking and moving is to set up unbreakable obstacles in a room: chairs, lamps, dresser, clothes pile, etc. Now have a conversation as you walk slowly around the room looking up at another person, or just pretend you are talking to someone. As you talk, avoid the obstacles without looking down at them. After a few minutes, move quickly (while still talking), then dance around, interacting with the obstacles. Make up different movement things to do and move the obstacles around.

Stage Design

Materials
3 large pieces of paper
Crayons, markers or watercolor paints
Ruler

Directions
Today it is your turn to design a set for a play. Like most set designers, the first step is to draw on paper what the set will look like and what furniture might be used. First, draw a stage outline making the stage wider at the front. Place the paper on the table so the front of the stage is facing you. This allows you to see it from the audience's point of view. Most plays have a few different sets. Decide on a story you like and think about the scenes the story might have. Draw set designs for a few scenes. If you have small plastic statues, try moving them around on top as you go over the story in your mind.

Ecology/
Environment

Composting

Materials
Leaves
Grass clippings
Food scraps
Potato peelings
Banana skins
Tea bags
Worms

Directions
More than half the trash your family throws away is organic and could be composted to turn it back into rich, fertile soil. There are several easy ways to compost. The simplest way is to make a pile of leaves and grass clippings in a corner of your yard. After a while, the bottom layers can be used as a rich mulch on your garden. Another way is to build a special bin made from wood posts and chicken wire. Place all your organic waste inside the bin, alternating with layers of soil. Keep it moist and turn it over every few weeks. Adding worms to your compost bin will help make an even richer and more fertile soil additive.

Note: Americans create about 1,200 pounds of organic garbage per year. For more information on composting, write to the Seattle Tilth Association, 4649 Sunnyside Avenue North, Room 120 Seattle, WA 98103. Email: tilth@seattletilth.org. Website: www.seattletilth.org.

Living Christmas Tree

Materials
Small or dwarf fir tree
Large clay pot
Potting soil

Directions
Go to your local nursery and select a tree that can be used as a Christmas tree—pine, fir, spruce, redwood, cedar, or hemlock. Plant your tree in a large clay or wood container, firmly packing potting soil around it. Keep your tree outside until just before Christmas, watering it regularly. When you bring your tree inside, put it by a window and away from heaters and fireplaces. Keep the soil moist by adding water or ice cubes. Place the pot on a flat tray to protect the floor or carpet. Decorate. After Christmas, place tree in the garage for a few days before taking it outside. Wait until spring to plant your tree. If you don't have the space to plant a tree, call your local park district and ask them where it could be planted. Save the container to use again next year.

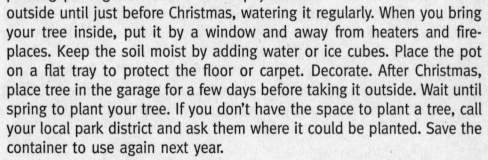

Note: For information about real Christmas trees and detailed caretips: www.realchristmastrees.org/treecare.html.

Recycling Assorted Paper

Materials
2 boxes or bins

Directions
You can recycle all kinds of
paper—cardboard, paper bags,

newspaper, and notepaper. Place cardboard from cereal and other boxes
(folded flat) in one box labeled "cardboard." In the other box, labeled
"paper," toss all other paper with the exception of shiny paper and
paper with plastic attached to it. Place newspapers in a pile and stack
paper bags sideways between the two boxes. Every week or two, tie the
newspapers and paper bags into small bundles and take them and the
boxes to the nearest recycling center. If you have a curbside recycling
service, place them at the curb weekly.

Note: Check out www.environmentaldefense.org for innovative, practical
ways to solve the most urgent environmental problems.

Recycling Bottles and Cans

Materials
Recycling box or bin

Directions
Soda cans and other aluminum products can be
ground down to small chips, melted, and turned into
solid aluminum bars from which new cans can be
made. To recycle cans, rinse them out and place in
a box or bin labeled "aluminum." Clean aluminum
foil, pie plates, and frozen food trays can be recycled
too. Pick up aluminum cans you find at school or on the ground and
take them home to recycle. Find out the location of the nearest recycling center or use the curbside recycling service if your neighborhood
has one.

Glass can be melted down in factories and mixed with new glass to make
new glass containers. To recycle glass bottles and jars in your home, find
a place you can keep three boxes for collecting glass. Label separate
boxes for brown, green, and clear glass. Remove the caps, corks, and
rings from the jars and bottles, but leave the paper labels on. Rinse the
glass out before putting it in the appropriate box.

Stop Junk Mail

Directions

1. Contact the Direct Marketing Association (DMA) and tell them you want to get off their list. On a postcard or letter, put the date, your name, your address, and sign it. (Include all variations of your name.) Tell them to remove your name from their mailing lists.

Direct Marketing Association
Mail Preference Service
P.O. Box 643
Carmel, NY 10512
Tel: 1- 212-768-7277
www.dmaconsumers.org

2. 1-800 No Thanks. As soon as you receive a publication in the mail you don't want, call the 1-800 number located somewhere on the piece and ask to be removed from the mailing list.

Note: Each year, junk mail destroys about eighty million trees, wastes twenty-eight billion gallons of water, and costs about $450,000,000 of your money to cart its promos, pleas, and promises to and from incinerators, garbage dumps, and recycling centers. That equates to about thirty-four pounds of junk mail for every man, woman, and child in the U.S. It's like stuffing a whole tree into our mail boxes every year. Go to www.ecocycle.org and click stop junk mail to find out more ways to stop junk mail.

Water Conservation

Directions

You can save up to 20,000 gallons of water a year by not letting the water run (that's enough to fill a swimming pool!). Here are some ways you can conserve water:

1. When brushing your teeth, just wet your brush, then turn off the water. Turn the water on again to rinse your brush.
2. When washing dishes, fill up the basin and rinse the dishes in it instead of running water over each dish and piece of cutlery.
3. When running a bath, plug the tub before you start.
4. For when you are thirsty, leave a bottle of water in the refrigerator instead of running water to fill your glass.

Note: Don't waste water by pouring it down the sink. Instead, pour it on a thirsty plant or top off your goldfish bowl. For more information about water conservation and more tips, go to www.wateruseitwisely.com.

Birdfeeder

Materials
Half-eaten fruits and vegetables
3 feet of string
Birdseed or cereal

Directions
Cut lengthwise grooves in the fruit or vegetable on all four sides. Cut the top off
about a half inch from the stem of the fruit.
Scoop out some of the insides of the apple
with a spoon, being careful not to break
the skin. Tie the string around it, criss-
crossing the string underneath and tying it above the top. Fill the center of the apple with birdseed or cereal. Hang the birdfeeder outside
where it will be protected from the rain.

Note: Try using lots of other half-eaten fruits for your birdfeeder—
orange, pear, nectarine—or vegetables such as a turnip, green tomato,
gourd, or firm squash.

Adopt-a-Stream

Materials
Garbage bag

Directions
Find a stream or creek in your area to adopt. Patrol the stream bank and pick up all the litter and trash. Place in a garbage bag and take home to throw away. Do not let your pet or your friends' pets leave their waste near the stream. Organize a party to plant native trees along the banks to curb erosion. If you notice oil, foam, suds, a bad smell, or a shiny film on the water, report it to a parent or other adult. If you find fish, bugs, and strong green plants in the water, that means the stream has plenty of oxygen and is healthy.

Note: For more information on "Save Our Streams," contact:
The Izaak Walton League of America,
707 Conservation Lane
Gaithersburg, MD 20878
Tel: (301)548-0150
     Toll Free: 1-800-IKE-LINE (453-5463)
Email: sos@iwla.org

Recycle Electronics

Directions

Computers

Many high schools and colleges have programs where students tear down computer equipment, upgrade the components, and then distribute the refurbished computers to schools and charities in need. Check your area for recycling programs before throwing away outdated comput-

ers. Most community recycling centers also have a pick-up day once or twice a year where you can drop off computers or electronics.

Cell phones

There are over one hundred fifty million retired cellular phones discarded in drawers and desks in the United States. Organize a cell phone drive and collect old phones to be recycled and donated to charitable organizations. Visit www.phones4charity.org to get started.

Note: For recycling programs in your state, visit the consumer education initiative website at www.eiae.org. For locations to dispose of rechargeable batteries and cell phones visit www.rbrc.org

Protect the Rainforests

Directions

Rainforests are home to more than half the world's plants and animals. It is estimated that they are being logged at the rate of 100 acres per minute! You can do many things to help save the rainforests:

1. Don't buy hamburgers made from beef raised on land that used to be rainforest. Ask where the beef comes from.
2. Don't buy products made out of tropical rainforest wood—rosewood, mahogany, teak, and ebony.
3. Read books from the library about rainforests and become informed.
4. Write to your US Senator and ask him or her to help protect the rainforests.
5. Organize a letter writing campaign at your school to stress the importance of protecting the remaining rainforests.

Note: To obtain more information about rainforests, go to www.ran.org where you can find a rainforest Pen Pal, find out about environmental changes caused by rainforest destruction, and learn about fuel efficient vehicles.

Use Rechargeable Batteries

Directions

Millions of batteries are thrown away each year. Most contain mercury, a lethal metal that can leak into the ground. Rechargeable batteries can be used over and over again. When they run down, you put them in a recharger which plugs into an electrical outlet. After it is recharged, the battery can be used again. Other ways to save batteries are:

1. Plug in portable CDs, tape players, and radios whenever you can instead of running them on batteries.
2. Use things that don't need batteries, such as solar calculators which obtain their energy from the sun.
3. Turn your flashlight or MP3 player off when not using it.

Note: Townships High School in New Jersey initiated a battery-recycling project, converting soda and laundry bottles into battery collection containers. Kids made up flyers for the school and community with details about battery drop-off, then arranged pick up with a recycling plant.

105

Taking a Stand

Directions

The best place to start saving the earth is at your school. Schools spend billions of dollars a year on textbooks, paper, and other supplies. Here are some ways you can take a stand:

1. Ask your teachers to use recycled paper only.
2. Use both sides of your note paper and insist that copying is done on both sides too.
3. Use recycled computer paper.
4. Request that paper towels, toilet paper, and other disposable paper are unbleached.
5. Write to textbook publishers and ask them to print on recycled paper.
6. Design posters about your environmental concerns and what students can do about them. Place them around your school.

Note: Initiate a regular column in your school newspaper featuring a school wide or specific environmental problem, and ways it can be solved by students and teachers.

Family

Contest Night

Directions

It's fun to play together as a family. Plan a family contest night full of fun competitions that everyone can participate in. Here are some ideas:

- Balance contest—you need two tin cans and a length of string. Set the cans two-feet apart, each person stand with one foot on the can, holding one end of the string in their hand. At the count of three, each challenger tries to unbalance their opponent by pulling on the string.
- The longest apple peel—you need an apple and a vegetable peeler. Each person peels an apple, then measure who has the longest unbroken peel.
- Coin spinning—see whose coin spins the longest. Make sure to give everyone a few practice spins.
- Blink test—stare at each other and see who blinks first.
- Laugh-a-thon—try to make opponents laugh by cracking jokes and making faces.
- House of cards—who can build the biggest house of cards.
- Jump rope—who can skip the longest.

Think of other things you could add to this list. Younger kids should get a point advantage so it is fair for everybody.

Family Newspaper

Materials
Strong paper
Felt pens
Pen
Glue
Photographs

Directions
Produce a newspaper about your family and its activities. Look at a local newspaper to get an idea of how to lay out the writing and pictures. Look at what sections they have: headline stories, special events, sports, house, and garden. Then add your own categories: holidays, family, friends, work, school, pets, and neighborhood news. Write your stories neatly in columns and use photographs or drawings. You may want to have an advertising or "help wanted" section. Be prepared to "interview" (that is, to ask people questions) to get information for your articles. Also, encourage others to write their own articles. Get the whole family to participate!

Midnight Feast

Materials
Feast food

Directions
This activity has to be done on a weekend or vacation when the family doesn't have to wake up for school or work. Someone needs to be the organizer of the feast. Decide on a place to have the feast: a backyard under the stars, in a fort you've made, the basement, or you could drive somewhere special. The place doesn't matter as long as it's kept secret until the last minute. Midnight is a magical time and this will be an adventure to talk about and remember for a long time. Plan food for the feast that the family doesn't get to eat often—nothing messy or difficult to carry. Get blankets to sit on and set the alarm clock for 11:45 so everyone can be awake and ready to meet and eat at 12 midnight.

Bubbles of Fun

Materials
Liquid dish soap
Bottle of glycerin
(get from a pharmacy)
Wire clothes hanger
Juice can
Broken sunglasses, plastic lids, or
any other circular object with no
center

Directions
To make the bubbles, put equal amounts of dish soap, water, and glycerin in a container and mix them together. Many things around the house will work to blow your bubbles through. Shape the wire hanger into a circle or square, dip it into a cake pan full of bubble liquid, and wave your arm in a big circle in front of you. Take a juice can, the little kind that has a place to drink out of the top, and cut the bottom out. Dip the bottom in the bubbles and blow from the top. Cut the inside of a plastic lid leaving the rim, hold it with a clothespin, and dip it in. Experiment with other bubble blowing devices that you make or find. Have everyone in the family create a bubble blower and have a bubble party!

Talent Show

Directions

In order to have a successful talent show, everybody in the family has to participate, even the family pet! If you have a small family, invite friends or relatives to participate. Talent comes in many forms: read a poem, play an instrument, do a dance, tell a joke, do a charade, act out an event from your week, sing a song, tell a personal story, stand on your head.

Do anything you want to express yourself. Give everyone a few weeks notice to get their acts together. Someone might want to write a program when all the acts have been decided. Whoever organizes the show is in charge of refreshments to eat between acts.

Note: This is a fun event to organize on a special holiday. Friends and relatives could participate in skits or personal performances.

Nonstop Talk

Materials
Kitchen timer or clock

Directions
The object of this game is to talk nonstop for one minute about a chosen subject. Everyone writes one or two subjects on a piece of

paper and puts them in a hat. Divide into two teams. You may want to have someone "referee" and watch the time. The referee picks a subject out of a hat, then announces, and the first player in team one starts talking. You are not allowed to repeat the same ideas and you must stick to the subject. If you slow down, your turn finishes automatically and the next person on your team speaks for a minute on the same subject. The referee keeps track of how long each player speaks. After team one has talked as long as they can, team two starts on a new subject. The winner is the team which has spoken for the longest time after all the seconds are added up.

Parents Day

Directions

Being a parent is hard work. It takes energy, time and lots of love! Parents need to see that their work is noticed, just like you do. Think of something special you could do for your Mom or Dad today to say "Thank-you. I love you and appreciate all the things you do for me." Here are a few ideas:

- Breakfast in bed
- A note left on their pillow at night
- Tea or coffee brought to them anytime
- The laundry folded
- A younger brother or sister's room cleaned
- Flowers or branches put in vases around the house
- Call a family meeting and ask the children to say what they appreciate about their parents
- Volunteer to do something without being asked
- Clean out the car
- Give a big hug and say "I love you"

Time Capsule

Materials
Airtight container

Directions
A time capsule is a container full of information about you, your family, and the times you live in. It gets buried in the ground to be discovered maybe hundreds of years from now. Think about the things you want to put in it: a letter about your life, pictures from magazines, today's paper, a CD with music and sounds, Velcro, an old calculator, or anything that people in the future might find interesting. Write the date you buried it somewhere. Bury the time capsule at least six inches underground and keep a record of where it is buried for yourself. You may want to put a rock on top of it and scratch in the words "time capsule" and the date.

Last Sentence

Directions

This is a group storytelling. Someone thinks of a last sentence like "Mrs. Smith danced all night," or "It was the first time he smiled," or

"No one would have thought he would do something like that." Start the story, then each person adds only one word. Keep the story going as long as you can until it seems right for the last sentence to be said. Think of another last sentence and play the game again.

Garage Sale

Materials
Stickers to mark prices
Pens and markers
Pieces of cardboard for signs
Tables or blankets to put things on
A cash box with $20 worth of change

Directions
This is a fun way to get rid of all the old stuff cluttering up your cabinets, closets, yard, and garage. You be the organizer. Have a family meeting and tell everyone your idea. Pick a day and give everyone a job. The jobs might be making posters for the adults to put on the street corners the day of the sale, marking prices, organizing what to sell, and cleaning out the garage. You may want to do some of these jobs all together. Each person is responsible for going through their own belongings and bringing sale items to a designated spot to be priced. On the day of the sale, put some music on. If it's sunny, move tables out into the yard and put a friendly smile on your face!

Note: You might have to sell things for less than the price marked—that's called bargaining. After the sale is over, donate what you didn't sell to a charity.

Map to Your House

Materials
Paper
Pencil, felt tip markers
Ruler

Directions
Make a map to your house for everyone in your family to use when having friends over. Investigate the roads and landmarks around your house. Show friends' houses, play centers, kindergartens, schools, local shops, parks, and whatever else is important to you. Take the ruler and begin drawing. Good luck!

Progressive Party

Directions

Organize this progressive dinner party with two or more other families. Each family makes one course of a meal: appetizer, soup, salad, main dish, and dessert. All the families meet at the first house for the first course then travel to each house until the meal is finished. It is fun to pick a theme like Mexican, Chinese, Italian, Barbeque, Fondue, Vegetarian, etc. Have everyone dress up, bring a piece of historical information, or sing a song in a different language, or each family could prepare some sort of entertainment. Use your imagination to make this a fun event each family will remember for a long time.

Field Trips

Whale Watching

Materials
Drawing paper
Pencil
Colored pencils
Binoculars

Directions
If you happen to live on the West Coast or visit California, Oregon, or Washington, you may be able to take a field trip to watch the Gray Whale migration. Over 20,000 Gray Whales migrate annually, making an 8,000 mile trip between their summer feeding grounds in Alaska and the winter breeding grounds of Mexico, the longest migration of any animal on the earth. The best months to watch them are March, April, and May. Seaside towns have tour boats that you can board for a fee. Take your drawing materials and binoculars. It will be a field trip you will always remember.

Note: Gray Whales were put on the Endangered Species list in 1971 and are protected by both the Marine Mammal Protection Act and the International Whaling Commission.

Performing Arts Rehearsal

Directions

Rehearsals of different kinds are going on all the time in most towns and cities. If you are interested in ballet, music, singing, plays, jazz, mime, children's theatre, or any other performing art, you can ask for permission to watch a rehearsal. To find out what is being produced, check the newspaper for announcements of auditions and for dates when opening nights are scheduled. To find out where to go to watch a rehearsal, call the company or group directly. Dress rehearsals are probably the best performances to watch because they move quickly with few delays. When you are at the rehearsal, remember to sit quietly and refrain from eating or drinking.

Note: Universities, high schools, and colleges are convenient places to watch rehearsals. Call the school for information and directions.

Television Station

Directions

Tours of television (and radio) stations are available by appointment only. Small groups are welcome and the tour usually takes 45 minutes to 1 hour. Call the television station in your area and ask for the promotions manager who will schedule your visit. Public television companies welcome visitors and are designed for public access. All main production areas have windows so that visitors can watch the personnel at work. You will see sets for weekly programs and also a teleprompter. You will also see the control studio where the signal is sent to the transmitter.

Radio stations also offer tours. They have a control studio where on-air personalities work, a newsroom, and a music library. You may be able to put a face to that disc jockey or radio announcer you have been listening to all this time!

Flea Market

Directions

A flea market is an interesting place to visit if you want to buy something or if you want to buy nothing. It consists of an open space filled with individual vendors selling used or almost new merchandise, as well as produce, plants, crafts, and food. Call the chamber of commerce or your public library for the location of the nearest flea market and for the days and hours it is open. Don't be surprised if you find just the thing you have been looking for!

You may wish to set up your own table at the flea market if you would like to sell toys, books, games, and items that you no longer use. There will be a fee and other conditions. Call and find out.

Note: Farmers' markets are also great places to visit. Take a roomy shopping bag and buy farm fresh fruits and vegetables, as well as jams, jellies, honey, eggs, and breads.

Art Museum

Directions

An art museum provides children and youth with a strong cultural and artistic focus. It has its own collection of artworks plus important local and regional exhibitions. Docents volunteer at many art museums and escort groups around the museum providing everyone with information and historical facts about the paintings and other works of art.  The docents at some museums prepare visitors with a slide presentation, particularly if there is a well-known artist or exhibition on display.

If you visit the art museum on your own and you like to draw, you can sit undisturbed and copy any of the works that you like. Take a drawing pad and some pencils with you. Art museums also have stores where you can purchase prints, books, postcards, and other items of interest.

Local Farm

Directions

Farm visits are popular with people of all ages. Some farms are specially adapted for visitors and have tours, open days, and visiting hours. Call the chamber of commerce or your public library for a farm near you. On the day of your visit, wear appropriate shoes (boots are best) and take a camera.

There are several kinds of farms you can visit: game farms where there will be wild animals and birds, pioneer farms where you will see how they farmed in the 1800's, dairy farms with milk cows and calves, vineyards, berry farms, and orchard farms with rows and rows of fruit trees and seasonal fruits.

Chocolate or Candy Factory

Directions

Not every city and town has a candy factory, but if yours does, call and see if you, your family, or a group can visit. Plan on taking 45 minutes to an hour to complete the tour. Candy-making is a very old skill and many of the things that you see will be "old-fashioned." For example, candy-

makers use copper tubs or urns in which to heat the candy and thick marble slabs on which to knead and shape the candy. You will see several different kinds of candy being made and if you visit a chocolate factory, you will see the many molds that are used to give chocolates their distinctive shape and design. The best parts of these field trips are the free samples at the end of the tour!

Zoo at Feeding Time

Directions

Zoos are usually open daily year-round, although the hours may be shorter during the winter months. The purpose of zoos is to enable people to see how wild animals behave in a natural  environment. Visitors to the zoo pay an entrance fee that goes toward the upkeep of the zoo. The best time to take your field trip is during feeding time. Food for the animals often comes from all over the world. Zookeepers and their assistants deliver the food to the animals according to established feeding schedules. You can call ahead to find out the mealtimes of certain animals so you can be on hand when the food is delivered. It is important to respect the animals and their right to eat undisturbed. Remember never to feed the animals because their diets are strictly controlled.

Note: The first zoo was built over 3,000 years ago in China. It was called the Garden of Intelligence.

Botanical Garden or Park

Directions

Most towns have some kind of garden, whether attached to a school, historical landmark, or as part of a city park. Plan to visit the park with a sketchbook in hand. Draw flowers, trees, bushes, or plants that interest you. Some gardens have the names of the plant listed on a label stuck into the ground. Write the name down so that when you  return home you can look it up and learn more about it. If you are lucky enough to find a gardener on duty, ask any questions that come to mind as you compliment the beautifully cared for garden.

Observatory

Directions

If you are interested in stars, planets, and constellations, an observatory or planetarium is the place to go. An observatory is a tall, dome-shaped building specially built to observe the night sky through large telescopes. Reservations are usually necessary to tour the facility and to look at the stars. The hours change according to the season and available daylight. Once you are inside, a tour guide will explain the different kinds of telescopes and answer your questions about astronomy. Plan to take your field trip at night. A planetarium, on the other hand, can show you the night sky any time of the day (as long as it is open to the public) because it is a closed dome with a light source inside and rotating projectors which simulate the changing night sky. Hopefully you will be able to recognize some constellations and bright stars on your own the next time you look up at the night sky from your home.

Note: In 1609, the Italian scientist Galileo first used a telescope to look at the skies. He observed that the earth moved around the sun which was contrary to what people believed at the time. They thought the earth was the center of the universe.

Cookie Factory

Directions

Cookie factories often cook over 2,000 cookies per hour! Check the Yellow Pages or call your public library to find the name and location of the nearest cookie factory or bakery. Tours are available for small and large groups and generally take about 30 minutes. You will watch all kinds of special equipment in action, including enormous mixers and ovens. Cookies drop onto a metal conveyor belt that passes through the oven, baking the

cookies in a matter of minutes. In other areas, you may see workers hand-decorating the cookies and packaging them. If you are in a bakery, you may see workers making bagels, rolls, and pastries. At the end of your tour, you will be invited to sample some of the baked goods. They may be still warm from the oven. Mmmmmm.

Airport

Directions

Airports are always fascinating places to visit. You do not need a guided tour to find out what is going on inside a busy airport. But did you know that most airports offer comprehensive

tours of their facilities? The tours usually take about one and a half hours and you will need good walking shoes. They often include a multimedia slide or video presentation before you begin walking. You may even have to ride an airport bus in order to see everything in and around the terminal. You can expect to visit the passenger services, baggage claim, control tower, and food services. Airports also feature artwork and historical collections, including exhibits from local and regional artists, studios, and museums. Your field trip can be tailored to suit your interests if you call ahead and let the tour manager know. Please note that tours are subject to change due to security restraints.

Ceramics or Art Studio

Directions

Check your community art center to find out if you have any practicing artists living in your community. You may be able to arrange a visit to the studio where you can watch the artist at work. Ceramics studios are especially fun because pots thrown on a wheel are formed quickly before your eyes. Many landscape artists paint at locations around town so you may  run into one without even planning a visit. Ask if you can sit and watch as the painting takes form.

Note: For a hands on experience with painting ceramics, look for a commercial studio in your community. Visit www.colormemine.com for locations.

Fitness

Jump Rope

Materials

Jump rope or clothesline rope, about 5 feet long

Directions

Jumping rope is excellent exercise and a great way to improve fitness. It is best done on a paved surface or on a gymnasium floor. To start jumping rope or to warm up, rock the rope back and forth instead of revolving it. This is called "Rock the Cradle." Now start revolving the rope, jumping with both feet together, keeping your arms wide. Try double jumps (turn the rope slowly), hopping on one foot then the other, revolving the rope in the opposite direction, running forward while turning the rope, and double turns (turning the rope quickly twice while jumping once).

Note: Contact "Jump Rope for Heart" to learn how you or your school can enter a fun jump rope competition.

Cross-Training

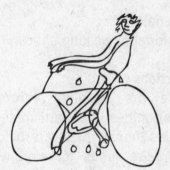

Materials
Bicycle
Roller blades (optional)
Running shoes
Jump rope

Directions
Cross-training is a great way to exercise if you like variety. If you like to train outdoors, it is best to cross-train on the weekends during the warmer months. Otherwise, use your school facilities or a nearby park. The idea is to get fit by combining three or four different aerobic activities. For example, you could jog for a mile, get on your bike and ride for three miles and then play basketball or tennis for 30 minutes. If you live near a swimming pool or somewhere you can swim, you could bike to the pool, swim laps for 20 minutes, bike home and then jump rope for 20-30 minutes. If you cross-train at a park, you could jog a mile, dribble a soccer ball for 20 minutes, put on your roller blades and skate for 20 minutes, and then do short sprints.

Note: Cross-training can be rigorous. Make sure you have parent and physician approval before you begin.

Walk-a-thon

Materials
Comfortable walking shoes

Directions
There are usually year-round opportunities to participate in "walk-a-thons." Most are held to help raise funds for worthwhile causes, e.g., American Cancer Society. Check the Community Activities section in your local newspaper to find out where and when. Meanwhile, start training! Begin by walking everywhere you can—do errands on foot, walk to school, leave your bike at home and walk to the store. During the weekends, take a longer walk (it helps to take a friend with you). Plan a three mile or five kilometer route near your home and keep track of the time it takes you to complete it. Before you know it, you will be in fine shape for the next "walk-a-thon" and many more after that.

Note: Walking is the oldest mode of human transportation. It is the activity that distinguishes us from other animals. Our bodies are specially designed for walking.

Bleacher Club

Directions

One good way to stay fit in the colder months (or any month) is to climb stairs. By far the best stair-climbing place is your school's football field. Except during football games, the bleachers are rarely used. Always warm up by stretching your calf and thigh muscles before attempting to climb the steps. You don't have to race; just keep an even pace, planting your foot squarely in the center of each step. Swing your arms and  keep your head up. Be gentle on your knees on the way down. If you don't have access to bleachers, you can get fit by climbing the stairs in a multi-story office building or by running up sand dunes.

Note: Stair-climbing can be rigorous. Make sure you have parent and physician approval before you begin.

Weightlifting

Materials
2-5 pound dumbbells
Inclined bench

Directions
Although lifting weights may not make you aerobically fit, it will give

you increased muscle tone and strength. Weightlifting exercises should be supplemented with sit-ups, push-ups, pull-ups, and other strengthening exercises. The idea is to strengthen as many large muscle groups as possible. There are many books on weightlifting which explain how to exercise each muscle group. With a minimum amount of equipment, you can start your weightlifting program at home in your garage. Here is an example exercise: using 2-5 pound dumbbells held palm upwards, you can do bicep curls by holding the elbow still and bending the forearm toward the shoulder and back, 12 times each arm. Do not overexert yourself and do not use weights over 5 pounds until you are over 14 years old. An inclined bench is necessary to exercise your shoulder, back, and chest muscles. Weightlifting will only strengthen your muscles if you do it regularly.

Note: It is not advised that children under 14 years undertake a rigorous weightlifting program. Their muscles and bones are not sufficiently developed.

Bike-a-thon

Materials
Bicycle
Helmet
Water bottle

Directions
Before you start getting fit on your bicycle, be sure to attend your local Bicycle Safety Program, usually sponsored by the Traffic Safety Department or your school's Parent Teacher Association. Find the bicycle trails in your area or the streets where bicyclists are safe. Start by bicycling a few miles a day and gradually increase the distance, especially during the weekends. When you are feeling fit, try hills and mountain trails. Always take a friend or an adult with you when bicycling far from home. If your bicycle has an odometer, keep a log of the miles you have biked and the time it has taken you.

Note: Take your bicycle in for an annual tune-up and safety check. Better still, borrow a bicycle book from the library and learn to do it yourself!

Fitness on Wheels

Materials
Roller blades or roller skates
Helmet
Protective pads for elbows,
wrists, and knees

Directions
Roller blading and skating are great ways to have fun and get fit at the same time. Choose a safe trail or sidewalk and gradually increase your distance. Always wear a protective helmet and pads.

Note: Ice skating is another way to enjoy staying fit.

Basketball Dribble

Materials
Basketball

Directions
Make an obstacle course outside using
outdoor furniture, small garbage cans,
or floor mats. Make sure there is space
between them. If indoors, clear a space

around the furniture or build your obstacle course in the garage. Dribble
the basketball around the obstacles, adjusting them to suit your ability
and fitness level. Try dribbling with the other hand or alternating hands.
Also try dribbling low and dribbling at waist height. You can even try
some of the fancy moves you see the professional basketball players use
when dribbling. When you are finished with your dribbling workout,
remember to put all the furniture and obstacles away or back where you
found them.

Bamma Runs

Materials
Masking or vinyl tape

Directions
Find an open floor space or flat area outside. Cut or tear off five pieces of tape in five foot (two meter) lengths. Make five parallel

lines about two yards, three yards, four yards and five yards apart. Stretch your leg muscles before starting. Run from the first line to the second line and run back to the start. Run from the first line to the third line and run back. Run from the first line to the fourth line and run back. Finally, run from the first line to the fifth line and run back. Each time you get to a line, you must touch it with both hands. To add to the challenge, you can do one or more push-ups when you get to each line.

Note: This running activity is named after a junior high school coach who had his players do it on the ten yard lines of the school's football field.

Aerobic Dance

Materials
Music player and cassette, or CD, or radio

Directions
Aerobic dance is an enjoyable and energetic way to get fit. Choose some music that has a good clear beat and is rhythmic. The music you choose should last from 10 to 20 minutes. Start by walking in place to the music to warm up. If you do not know any dance moves, you can jog in place, jump forward and backward, hop on one foot and then on the other, and do jumping jacks. Put them all together in a sequence that you can repeat. Write it down later so you can remember it for next time. To learn new aerobic dance moves, you can watch an aerobic class on TV or ask your PE teacher at school. Continue to add variety and challenge to your aerobic routine and soon you will look forward to your afterschool aerobic dance session.

Note: Aerobic activity significantly increases the oxygen supply to the heart, lungs, and all other body parts.

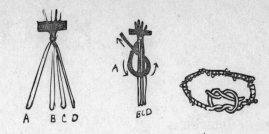

Friendship

Pen Pals

Directions

How would you like to have a friend in a foreign country? Would you like to hear about their schools, what they like to do, the foods they eat, and what their families are like? A pen pal is someone you can become friends with through the mail. You can learn all about their lives and they can learn about yours. Make sure you send a picture and your complete address in your first letter.

Organizations to write to get a pen pal:

American Kids Pen Pal Club
P.O. Box 2
Elizabeth, AR 72531
Write a little about yourself,
if you want a boy or girl pal,
and from what country. Cost: $2.00

Peace Links Pen Pals for Peace
747 Eighth St. SE
Washington, DC 20003
For Russian Pen Pals
Cost: Free

Friends Around the World
P.O. Box #10211
Merrillville, IN 46411-0266
Cost: $3.50

Pressed Flower Card

Materials
Heavy paper
Glue
Tweezers
Pressed flowers
Felt tips
Ruler

Directions
Collect flowers from your yard, park, forest, roadside, or neighborhood. Make sure you only take a few and never take a flower if there is only one in the ground. Flowers that are small and delicate work best because they press flat. Some of the prettiest ones are wildflower weeds! Once you collect your flowers, press them between heavy books (save old phone books for this), then give the flowers a few days to press and dry out. Design your card (you may want to make a few at a time). Look at poetry books to get ideas of what to write inside. When you are ready to glue the flowers to the card, use the tweezers to take one flower at a time out of the books. Put glue on the card where the flower will go. Place the flower on the card using the tweezers. Then put a clean cloth over the top and delicately press the flower down. Continue adding flowers until you like the design.

Note: You can also glue pressed flowers to candles and glass vases and coat with a clear acrylic.

Kidnap Breakfast Surprise

Directions

If one of your friends has a birth-day or is celebrating a great accomplishment, plan to kidnap them for breakfast one morning to help them celebrate. First, call your friend's parents to let them know you will be coming early in the morning. Arrange for a parent to drive you and a few other

friends to the person's house. Drag them out of bed and make them go to breakfast in their pajamas. Put a sign on them that says "It's my birth-day" or "I made the swim team!" or whatever event you are celebrating.

Fortune Cookies

Ingredients
4 eggs
½ cup melted butter
½ cup rice flour
¾ cup sugar
Pinch of salt
2 tablespoons water
Baking tray, mixer, or hand beater

Directions
Write messages of fortune on pieces of paper that might relate to things in your friend's lives. Preheat oven to 350°F (180°C). Grease the baking tray well. Separate the egg whites from the yolks. Beat the egg whites for several minutes until they stand up in points. Stir in the rice flour, sugar, and salt and beat the mixture well for another two minutes. Add the melted butter and water, then beat everything together until the mixture is like thin cream. Put spoonfuls of the mixture on the baking tray leaving plenty of room between them. Bake for 8 minutes or until the edges are turning brown. Lift one at a time off the cookie tray. Working as quickly as you can, put a message in the center and fold it (see illustration). If the cookies start to harden put them back in the oven for a minute. Give them to your friends in secret.

Friendship Bracelets

Materials
Embroidery thread
Tape
Scissors

Directions
There are many different ways to make knotted friendship bracelets. All of them contain similar knots and take very little time to learn. This bracelet has only one knot to learn called a spinning spiral.

1. You will need four different colored strings each thirty inches long.
2. Tie the strings together with a knot about five inches from the top.
3. Tape the short ends to the tabletop and begin to do the spinning spiral knot as shown below.

When you make a spinning spiral always knot from the left. Put A over B, C, and D, then under B, C, and D, holding B, C, and D tightly as you pull A. Use string A until you have one and a half inches of knots. Then switch to string B going over A, C, and D, follow with C and D in the same way. Tie a knot when finished as shown.

Note: This is a fun travel activity. It is also a great group party activity.

Have a Debate

Directions

Get a group of friends together and have a debate. That means you pick a subject of interest to everyone and talk about it. It could be something silly like "dogs are more intelligent than cats," or it could be serious like "how to get homeless people off the streets," or it could be personal like "what would you do if you had to move?" The object is to let everyone express their opinions, each person listening, without one person doing all the talking. If you exhaust one topic, move on to another.

Sounds Embarrassing

Materials
Piece of scrap fabric
Scissors
Balloon

Directions
It is so much fun to laugh and it seems friends can usually take a joke! Here are two tricks to bring on the giggles.

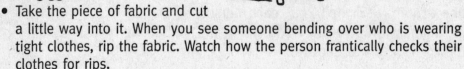

- Take the piece of fabric and cut a little way into it. When you see someone bending over who is wearing tight clothes, rip the fabric. Watch how the person frantically checks their clothes for rips.
- Blow up a balloon halfway. Try to hide the balloon under your clothes or hide behind a couch or chair. Wait for someone to sit down, sneeze, cough, or lift something, then let a sudden spurt of air out of the balloon!

Mind Reading

Materials
Plain index cards or blank paper
Pencil or markers

Directions
Do you think it's possible to read someone's mind? Some people have the ability to send messages from their brain to another person's brain without words or signs. We don't quite know how this is done. It may be that the human brain has a way of signaling that we have not developed or have forgotten how to use. Play this game with a friend to see if you can read each other's minds. Draw five simple shapes on the paper or cards, like a dog, cat, tree, house, flower, tree, apple, bird, etc. Now one of you place the cards face down in front of you. Turn one card over and look at it. Then close your eyes and think of nothing else. The other person closes his or her eyes and tries to have a blank mind to receive the message. The receiver draws the shape that comes to mind on a piece of paper. Try it a few times in a row, then switch being receiver and sender.

Gift Basket

Materials
Small or large basket
Ribbon
Card
Goodies for inside the basket

Directions
Gift baskets can be small or large and they can contain anything you like. They can be a birthday present or just a cheering up present. They can have bought items or handmade items. They contain any mixture of things you think the person might like. Find or buy a basket and decorate it with a ribbon. Now the fun starts—fill it up, deliver it to the person, and watch them smile! Some things to put in the basket: baked goods (cookies, muffins, bread), tea or specialty coffee, fruit, flowers, soap, lotion, bath goodies, trading cards, framed pictures, your own work of art, handmade stationery, jams and jellies, favorite magazines, golf balls, school pencils and notebooks, hair stuff, candles.

Guess Who?

Directions

Call one of your friends and say, "My voice is disguised, can you guess who this is?" Below are a few ways to easily disguise your voice.

- Hold a cloth over the phone mouthpiece.
- Shape your lips like you are about to whistle, then talk and keep your lips frozen in that shape.
- Hold your nose while you are speaking.
- Smile widely, curling your lips back to show your teeth.

Special Wishes

Materials
Piece of cardboard
Crayons, markers, or paint
Yarn or string
Scissors
Glitter, stickers, etc.

Directions
Cut the piece of cardboard in the shape of
a star. Decorate the front of the star in an
interesting design. On the back of the star,
write a wish or a thought you would like one of your friends to have.
For example, "I wish you to be the best actor at the play audition," "I
hope you make it through the spelling test and get an A," "You are
charming, funny, and kind," "I hope you hit a home run!" Sign your
name if you want, or if you want it to be a secret, write "from your
secret friend." Poke a hole in the top of the star, run the piece of string
through, and tie at the top so it hangs like an Olympic medal. Hang it
in the friend's locker or place it over their coat at lunch.

Make a Friend

Directions
Is there anyone in your class that seems to sit alone, play alone, or walk home alone? Decide to introduce yourself and ask her or him to play with you. This can be very hard to do so practice in front of a mirror a few times. If you are the person that is always sitting alone, you can make a friend—you just have to be brave. Take a few days to observe the kids in your class, then pick someone who seems friendly. Ask your mom, dad, brother, or sister to "role play" (that means act out a part) with you. They can be the friend you want to make and you can be yourself. Practice different words to use. Sometimes practice makes the actual encounter less scary. There are many people who find it hard to make friends, so keep trying and don't give up, because having a friend is very special.

Games

Pick-Up Sticks

Materials
30 wooden skewers
Colored paint or felt pens—black,
red, blue, green, and yellow

Directions
To make your set of pick-up sticks,
paint the ends of the skewers with
the following colors: one black, three
red, five blue, nine green, and twelve
yellow. Assign points to each color as follows: black ten points, red five
points, blue three points, green two points, and yellow one point. Use
a table or the floor to play the game. Hold the sticks upright in a bunch
in one hand just above the floor or table. Release the sticks and let
them fall. Now try to remove the sticks one by one without moving any
other stick in the pile. You can use the black stick to help you remove
other sticks. Continue removing sticks until you move another stick by
mistake. Now count the value of your sticks. Play the game again and
see if you can beat the number.

Note: Pick-up sticks probably originated in China where the sticks were
carved out of ivory and were elaborately decorated.

Sardines

Directions

This game is a variation of "hide and seek." It is best played outdoors. "Sardines" can be played with two or more players. One player is "it" and he or she goes off to hide while the other players count to 100 by 2's or 5's. When the other players have finished counting, they call out, "coming ready or not!" (or something similar to warn the player who is hiding). Everyone goes off to find "it," seeking separately. As each player finds "it," he or she hides in the same space, until finally, all the players are squeezed into the hiding place. The first player to find "it" becomes "it" for the next game.

Marbles

Materials
Chalk
1 shooter, 8-10 marbles

Directions
Draw a circle about two feet in diameter on a flat surface (or if indoors, tape a circle on the carpet). Draw (or tape) another circle about six feet in diameter outside the first circle. Place two or three marbles (per player) in the center of the inner circle. Stay behind the outside circle and place the "shooter" marble behind the outside circle. Shoot it towards the marbles in the center and try to knock as many as possible out of the inner circle. The "shooter" must stay within the inner circle. If you have knocked one or more marbles out of the inner ring, you can retrieve the "shooter" and take another turn. Continue until you miss. The winner is the one with the most marbles after all are shot from the inner ring.

Note: "Bombardier" is a variation. Place ten marbles in the center, stand up, and drop your "shooter" into the pile. See how many you can knock out of the inner ring this way!

House of Cards

Materials

1 or 2 packs of playing cards

Directions

This is a great activity for rainy days.
You will need a flat surface that no one
will disturb. The idea is to build a house

of cards which uses up all the cards in the packs. You cannot bend, staple, roll or mutilate the cards in any way. Start with a simple structure of four cards in a box shape and add a roof. Keep working outwards and upwards, adding more cards and more creativity. With patience and care you will soon have built a mansion or perhaps the Great Wall of China! Take a photo of your structure if you are particularly proud of it.

Note: You can also build houses with dominoes, Legos, Monopoly cards, and sports cards.

Hopscotch

Materials
Chalk

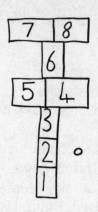

Directions
There are a number of ways a hopscotch game can be set up. Find a level surface and draw the diagram shown on this page. Each box should be about eighteen inches square. Draw another line a few feet from the bottom of the diagram. Number each box as shown. You will need a smooth stone or other small object that can be thrown onto the squares. To start the game, stand behind the line and throw the stone into square 1. Hop over the stone onto square 2 and continue to hop to square 3. Jump with both feet landing on squares 4 and 5, hop onto square 6, and jump with both feet onto squares 7 and 8. To come back the other way, jump and turn at the same time and retrace your steps. When you reach square 2, stand on one foot and bend down to pick up your stone. Return to the line. Continue the game by throwing your stone onto square 2 and repeating the hopping, jumping, and turning. You lose your turn when you miss the square with your stone or when you step on or over a line. Leave your stone in the square to be repeated if you are playing with friends. Try to complete the path through the hopscotch from square 1 to square 8 and back again.

Tug-o-War

Materials
Thick rope

Directions
Tug-o-war is best played in teams, although two children can have a try if they are about the same age. It is a game of strength and endurance. The

teams should be evenly matched and they line up facing each other, holding on to opposite ends of a long rope. A marker is placed exactly halfway between the team leaders. On a signal, the rope is first tightened and everyone gets into position. Someone says, "Ready, set, go" and each team tries to pull the other over the middle marker. The team that pulls the opposing leader over the marker wins.

Note: According to the laws of physics, it's not the pulling on the rope that makes the difference, it's the pushing of the feet against the ground (Newton's 3rd Law).

Wall Ball

Materials
Tennis ball
Wall

Directions
This is a game for one or two players. The idea is to throw and catch the ball according to a sequence of tasks. When you miss, you lose your turn and have to start all over the next time. Here are some tasks:

Meensies: Throw the ball and catch it before it bounces—10 times

Onesies: Throw the ball and catch it after one bounce—9 times

Clapsies: Throw the ball and clap hands before you catch it—8 times

Kneesies: Throw the ball and touch your knees before catching it—7 times

Twosies: Throw the ball and catch it after two bounces—6 times

Under the knee: Lift your leg and throw the ball under the knee before catching it—5 times

Highsies: Throw the ball as high as you can before catching it—4 times

Touch the ground: Throw the ball and catch it after touching the ground—2 times

Turn around: Throw the ball and catch it after turning completely around—1 time

Note: After going through the sequence without missing, go through again using the right hand only, then with the left hand only.

Clock Solitaire

Materials

Pack of cards (without the Joker)

Directions

Shuffle the cards and then deal out twelve cards face down in a circle like a clock. Place one card in the center. Deal another twelve cards on top of the first ones and place the next card in the center. Repeat. Deal another twelve cards, but keep the spare card. Turn this card

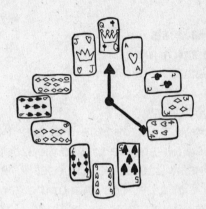

up and place it under the hour of the clock it represents. Jack is eleven and Queen is twelve. Take a card from the top of that pile and place it where it belongs. If you pick a King, you place it under the center pile. Continue until there are four Kings in the center, and therefore, no more cards to place on the clock. To win you must have all the cards face up on the clock.

Note: Playing cards originated many hundreds of years ago in both China and Europe. Some of today's card games are over 600 years old!

161

Tic-Tac-Toe

Materials
Scratch paper
Pencil or pen

Directions
Draw the tic-tac-toe diagram (two
vertical lines and two horizontal
lines). One player chooses X and
the other O. The idea of the game

is to have three Xs or three Os in a straight line, either vertical, horizontal or diagonal before your partner does. X always starts first and puts an X in any of the boxes. O then takes a turn and tries to prevent X from winning or tries to place Os in the right places.

Note: To increase the challenge, draw a diagram with sixteen squares and try to place four Xs or Os in a straight line.

Penny Pitching

Materials
Pennies, beads, or small rocks
A wall
Chalk

Directions
Start this game by drawing boundaries
next to a wall and away from it, about
four feet apart and six feet long. Draw another line at the top of the
playing area. To start the game, the first player stands behind the line
and throws a penny against the wall. The next player throws his or her
penny against the wall and tries to hit the other player's penny. If he or
she succeeds, that player takes both pennies. The player who has just
won pitches the next penny. The game is continued until one player
winds up with all the pennies.

Note: Variations for this game include winning only if the pennies land
on top of each other, drawing boxes that the pennies must land inside,
and throwing pennies with the object of landing closest to the wall in
order to win all the pennies.

Horse

Materials
Basketball
A hoop

Directions
This game is best played with
two players, but more players
works okay too. First, decide on the order of turns. The first player then
attempts any kind of shot. If he or she misses, the second player
becomes the "leader." If he or she makes the shot, the other players
must make the exact same shot. If the following player misses, the first
player gets the letter H and the next player is the new "leader." The
game continues until one player has accumulated all the letters of
HORSE. That player is the winner.

Visualization Game

Materials
Assorted objects
Tray
Tea towel
Small sack
Paper and pencil

Directions
Collect ten to twenty small common objects, e.g., safety pin, spoon, eraser, watch, comb, button, ring, thumb tack, clothespin, key, cork, stamp, etc. Place the objects on a tray. The players have one minute to look at the tray and then it is covered with the tea towel. The players must then write down all the objects they can remember. The winner is the one who has the most correct items.

This game can also be played by using the sense of touch. Place the objects in a small sack (burlap is best) with only enough room at the opening for a hand to go through. Each player has one minute to place his or her hand in the bag and then try to recognize as many objects as possible. Again, the player who has written down the most correct items is the winner.

Hobbies

Flower Arranging

Materials

Flowers and branches
Vase, dish, or other container
Dry foam
Scissors or garden shears
Adhesive clay
Florist spikes (to hold foam in place)

Directions

Prepare the chosen container by attaching a florist spike to the bottom of the container with adhesive clay. Push the dry foam onto the florist spike. Prepare the flowers so they last as long as possible.

- Cut the stems at an angle to expose more stem to the water.
- Strip any leaves or branches that would be underwater.
- Remove thorns to make stem easier to handle.
- With a knife or scissors, scrape the lower end of the stem to encourage it to take up water.
- For woody stems, hammer the end of the stem on a wooden board, then make cuts straight up from the bottom.

Fill container with water adding a few drops of bleach and a teaspoon of sugar to the water. Arrange the flowers in the container as creatively as you like. If you need ideas, get a book on flower arranging—the pictures are beautiful.

Pets

Materials
Book on your selected pet

Directions
Here are a few things to consider before getting a pet:

- Care of a pet is a long-term commitment, so ask yourself if you will still enjoy your pet one year from now.
- A pet demands time, so take your school work and extra activities into consideration when choosing which pet to get.
- A pet requires an ongoing financial commitment: purchase cost, food, licensing fees (dogs), veterinary bills, and pet-care products.

Some pets that are low-cost, low-time, and easy to care for are birds, goldfish, and turtles. Guinea pigs, rabbits, and cats take a bit more care. Dogs take the most care because they need exercise and companionship as well as daily care. Read as much as you can about your prospective pet and remember that it will be your responsibility, not your parents,' so be ready to do all the jobs your pet requires.

Photography

Materials
Camera
Film

Directions
If you like looking at people and at the world, if you would like to record what you see in a creative way, if you like to tell stories, then photography is for you. There are many things to learn so go to the library and check out a beginning photography book. Once you know how to use your camera, here are a few projects to try:

- Panorama view—this is a long strip of photos put together that show one view. First stand on a spot where you can see the whole view. Start from the farthest point on the left and take the first photograph. Keep the camera level and the horizon at the same height as you move the camera to the right. Make sure you have about a third of your first picture in the viewfinder before you take the next photo. Keep taking overlapping photographs until the whole scene has been shot.
- Make your own cards out of thick cardstock and glue pictures on front.
- Start a photo diary containing pictures of people you meet, places you visit, friends, etc. Stick each picture in the book and write underneath all the information about the picture you can think of.
- A day in the life of your family—follow family members around all day taking pictures of what they do.

Cooking

Directions

What is your favorite food to eat? Why not become a specialist in making that type of food? There are all sorts of cookbooks in the library specializing in food of different countries like China, Italy, France, Mexico, Greece, or Japan. There are also cookbooks that specialize in kinds of cooking like breads, desserts, soup, pasta, and many others. To begin your research, pick your area of specialization then find a book or DVD that has pictures. Ask a parent to help you if the recipe is difficult or if you need special ingredients. You may be able to find a cooking class to take. Ask a local restaurant if you could watch the chef. The possibilities are endless. The best part is that after all your hard work you get to eat the results!

Collecting

Directions

Collections come in all shapes and sizes. Some kids collect general categories like "all stamps," others collect specialized areas like "stamps from England." There are theme collections like collecting anything that has to do with teddy bears. Some collections are very cheap and some cost money. The most important

thing to consider when deciding what to collect is how much it interests you. Here are some ideas: stamps, postcards, swap cards, photos, autographs, buttons, coins, earrings, key chains, badges, marbles, magnets, toys, dolls, figurines, shells, stones, leaves, feathers, insects, butterflies, pine cones, matchbox cars, trains, ships, models, bottles, teacups, balls, hats.

Dance

Directions

There are many forms of dance such as hip-hop, jazz, ballet, modern, folk, square, tap, ballroom, break dancing, and just plain creative dance. Each form of dance has a history, certain movements that distinguish it from other forms of dance, dance troops that perform, and classes offered. Find some form of dance you like. There are books you can look at, videotapes that demonstrate steps and classes you could take (sometimes you can take the first class free to see if you like it). Get in front of a mirror, turn on some music, and practice the steps you have learned, then try to make up some of your own! Tell your parents about your new interest and maybe they will take you to see a performance or enroll you in a class!

Jigsaw Puzzles

Materials
Jigsaw puzzle
Big sheet of cardboard

Directions
Find a puzzle you like that is at your level—not too many pieces, but not too easy either. Spread the pieces colored side up on the sheet of cardboard. Find the four corner pieces, then all the straight edges. Put the side pieces together, then group the rest of the pieces together by color. Put the puzzle together bit by bit. The cardboard piece allows you to move the puzzle wherever you want.

Note: Garage sales and flea markets are good places to get puzzles at bargain prices—just be aware there could be a few pieces missing.

Illustration

Materials
Children's picture books
Paper
Pencil
Felt tip markers or watercolor paint

Directions
Illustrators draw pictures for books. If you like to draw, here is a good hobby for you. Look at all sorts of picture books and notice how the illustrator

has drawn and colored the pictures. Ask yourself what you like about them and what you don't like. Notice the different drawing style each illustrator has. Try to copy styles you like, not by putting a paper over the top and tracing, but by looking at it and then copying the lines and shapes onto your page. Looking and copying trains the eye to see shapes and teaches the hand to get those shapes onto paper. Your illustrations probably won't look anything like the books because you draw them in your own style just like the illustrator did. Illustrate a book of your own. You only need a sentence or two on each page. Make sure the illustration says something the words DO NOT say.

Hiking

Materials
Backpack
Hat
Sunscreen
Tennis shoes or hiking boots

Directions
If you like being outside and looking at trees, flowers, birds, mountains, fish, streams, rocks, and earth, you will like hiking.

Most places have hikes of some sort available. Big cities have large parks and there are guide books available that outline hiking trails outside the city. You may have to ask one of your parents or an older sibling to take this hobby up with you since wandering around alone is not a good idea. You can do all the research and planning for your hikes by checking at local libraries for books on family hikes in your area. Community centers or scouting groups may also be of some help. You will want to take food and water in your backpack as well as sunscreen. This may be a good time to learn how to use a compass. You may even be able to carry your sleeping bag and tent and camp out. Happy trails!

Listen to Music

Directions

Music comes in many different styles: classical, jazz, modern, pop, rap, hard rock, soft rock, and folk. It is fun to listen to different music to see what you like. Usually you can find all sorts of stations on the radio. You can also check out CDs at the library. There are many books on different music styles, so once you find one you like, find out more about it. Music has to be listened to in order to be appreciated, so start listening. Write down the pieces you like and keep a record of the tapes or CDs you have listened to. After a while you will know what music you like the best.

175

Learn a Sport

Directions

Is there a sport you like to watch or play that you don't know much about? There are all sorts of interesting things to learn: the history of the sport, rules, star players, how to play, and what equipment to use. You can learn these things from books, by asking questions, or by watching the sport being played. It helps to tell the people

you live with that you are taking a special interest in something new. Family members can help by pointing out newspaper or magazine articles or maybe even going on a trip to a sporting event with you!

Build Forts

Materials
Wood scraps
Tin
Old furniture
Blankets
Branches

Directions
Explore your yard for possible fort locations. Build your fort with whatever you can find. Maybe you have a tree in which you could build a tree house. When you are bored with one location, take your fort down and move to a new one. Make a point to collect good fort materials and put them where they won't get thrown out. You might want to have a fort notebook and draw or take a picture of each of the forts you make. Take your fort building seriously—who knows, you may become an architect!

Explore Old Buildings

Directions

Look around your community for interesting old houses or buildings. Sometimes cities have a historical society or a town museum where you can go and look at pictures of buildings as they stood 100 years ago. Sketch pictures of the old buildings in a notebook, try to find out the year they were built, and any local history. Bring

along a digital camera to note architectural design elements; molding, arches, porches, gardens, or stairways. You may also want to look at architecture books in the library to compare the building you are looking at with other buildings built around the same time. Many historical buildings offer tours certain times during the year. Call your town hall to find out what is available.

Horticulture

Flower-Press

Materials
Heavy cardboard or plywood
Flat coffee filters
String or wide elastic

Directions
First make the flower-press out of
the cardboard or plywood. Cut two
pieces twelve inches square. Place
one on top of the other to make sure they fit neatly together. Cut two
lengths of string or elastic (twenty-four inches). Gather flowers from your
garden or when you are out on a nature walk. Keep them undisturbed until
you get home. Place a coffee filter, opened flat, on the cardboard and carefully spread one or two flowers on it. Place another filter on top. Repeat
until you have used up the flowers. Now place the other piece of cardboard
on top. Tie securely with the string or elastic. You may need someone else
to help you hold the layers down. Place the flower-press in a cool, dry
place for several days. Gently open it to view or remove your dried,
pressed flowers.

Herb Garden

Materials
Assorted herb seeds
Small clay flower pots
Potting soil
Popsicle sticks

Directions
Fill the pots three-fourths full with pot-
ting soil. Pour water on top to moisten the soil. Sprinkle five or six seeds
on top of the soil and lightly cover with more potting soil. Label popsicle
sticks with the name of the herb and insert sticks in the appropriate pots.
Place pots on a window ledge. They will not take long to germinate. Keep
the soil moist. After the herbs are a few inches high, they can be snipped
and added to food dishes. Later, the herb plants can be transferred to the
garden. Good herbs to include are lemon balm, mint, parsley, chives,
thyme, basil, and scented geraniums.

Note: If popsicle sticks are not available, cut narrow strips from a
plastic milk carton. Make pointed ends and label with an indelible
marking pen.

Bulbs for Spring

Materials
5 or 6 daffodil or tulip bulbs
Shallow clay flower pot
Potting soil
Pebbles

Directions
Fill the bottom of the pot with
small pebbles. Arrange the bulbs,
pointed end at the top, on the
pebbles. Cover with potting soil
and press it firmly around the bulbs. Moisten soil with water. Place the
pot in a cool, dark place for several weeks or until the tips emerge.
Bring into the sunlight. The plants should bloom in about a month. If
planted in the fall, there will be blooms in the winter or early spring.
After their blooming season, plant them out in the garden.

Note: Other bulbs to try are crocuses, hyacinths, and freesias.

Wildflower Garden

Materials
Packet of wildflowers

Directions
Find a neglected area of the garden or a bare area of roadside. Rake the soil and pull out any weeds. Water generously. When buying the seeds, make sure the selection is appropriate for the climate and area where you live. Follow the directions on the wildflower  seed packet. Visit the site often to water and to control the bugs by handpicking them off the plants. After they have finished blooming, allow the plants to go to seed. That way there will be a fresh new crop of wildflowers next year!

Bean Teepee

Materials
Packet of pole bean seeds
Long stakes or bamboo

Directions
Prepare an area of soil about six
feet square. Arrange the stakes in
a teepee shape, placing them in
the ground six inches from the
edge of the soil area and meeting in the middle overhead. Secure the
tops of the stakes together with string. Soak the bean seeds overnight.
Plant the seeds according to the packet directions around the base of
the teepee on the outside. Water generously. As the beans begin to
grow tall, tie the stems carefully to the stakes. In six to eight weeks, the
bean plants will cover the stakes and you can play inside the teepee.
The beans can be eaten fresh or harvested and cooked.

Note: Scarlet runner beans are a good choice. They have bright red flowers and tasty, flat green pods. Other pole bean varieties work just as
well.

Berry Patch

Materials
Assorted berry plants—raspberry, strawberry, blueberry

Directions
Most berry plants thrive with very little work. Blueberries are native American plants which easily adapt to gardens. Buy rooted canes of raspberry, loganberry, and other edible berries and plant two to three feet apart. Berry shrubs in containers will bear berries the first season. Also buy strawberry plants. Plant in well-drained soil in sun to light shade. Strawberries need room to spread on the surface of the soil. All berry plants need regular watering, especially during flowering and fruiting.

Note: The berry shrubs may need sturdy posts with wires tied between them after they are a few years old.

Cuttings

Materials
Potting soil
Sand
Pot with drainage holes
Glass jar

Directions
New plants can be grown from cuttings. Prepare the soil by mixing sand with potting soil, the more sand the better. Put mixture in the pot and run water through. The better the pot drains, the better the cuttings will grow. Choose healthy, normal twigs or stems and use a sharp knife to cut a four- to five-inch length, making the cut just below a leaf. Remove all leaves on the lower half of the cutting. Insert the cutting to half its length in the pot. Place several cuttings in one pot. Invert a glass jar over the cuttings to minimize water loss. Keep out of direct sunlight until rooted. Wait until the rooted cuttings are growing well before moving them into individual pots or containers. Remember to keep soil moist.

Note: Softwood cuttings root more quickly and easily than hardwood ones. For better starts, dip cuttings in rooting hormone before inserting in pot.

Rock Garden

Materials
Rocks
Soil
Assorted rock plants

Directions
Find a sunny spot in the garden or out-side, about one square yard (meter). Arrange the rocks in a creative or pleasing mound or as a border, leaving space between them for soil and plants. Half

fill the spaces with soil and press firmly into all the nooks and crannies. Water carefully and thoroughly. Add and subtract rocks where the water is running out to make the rock garden watertight. The best plants to put in the rock garden are small or tiny shrubs, miniature bulbs, and annuals and perennials that form low tufts of leaves and flowers. In mild climates, plant succulents and cacti. After planting, add more soil and press firmly. Keep lightly watered and remove weeds as they appear.

Note: Examples of rock garden plants are sedum, phlox, veronia, crocus, alyssum, muscari, primula, viola, and sempervivum.

Off-Beat Garden

Materials
Roly-poly squash
Gourds
Allium gigantium
Chinese lantern
Venus flytrap
Spaghetti squash
Sunflower
Pampas grass
Peanut plant
Date palm

Directions
The off-beat garden can be designed for outdoors or indoors. Choose one to three varieties that interest you. Prepare the soil according to the plants' requirements. If starting from seed, plant in pots and keep moist. When seeds germinate and are strong, transplant to a permanent location. Some of the plants grow very tall, like the sunflower, date palm, and allium gigantium, so be prepared!

Avocado Tree

Materials
Avocado seed
Sharp nail
3 round toothpicks
Tumbler

Directions
Pierce the avocado seed with the nail
to make three holes evenly spaced
around the middle of the seed. Insert
a toothpick in each hole. Fill the tum-

bler with water and balance the avocado seed on the top, making sure
the bottom of the seed is in the water. Place on a window ledge. Soon
it will begin to produce a root and a shoot. As soon as the shoot has
a few leaves, snip off the top ones to encourage the plant to branch
out. Pot the little tree when the roots are thick. If you live in a warm
climate, you can plant the tree outside. Remember to keep it watered.

Note: The avocado is an evergreen tree which can grow to thirty feet.
There are two main kinds—Mexican and Guatemalan. The botanical
name is Lauracaea.

Hanging Baskets

Materials
Hanging wire basket
Sphagnum moss
Potting soil
Selected plants (see Note)

Directions
Hanging baskets of flowers provide lots of color throughout the summer and fall. A ten-inch basket will hold eight to twelve plants, depending on the varieties chosen. Pack the sphagnum moss around the inside of the basket. Soak in a deep basin or bucket. Drain. Half fill with moist potting soil. Place taller plants in the center and spreading plants around the outside. Fill with potting soil and press down firmly. Water one more time before hanging. As the plants grow, they will need more frequent watering. Water until water runs out of the bottom. Remove dead flowers by pinching them off at the stem.

Note: Hanging container plants include geranium, vinca, marigold, viscaria, petunia, begonia, phlox, verbena, nemesia, nasturtium, lobelia, portulaca, ivy, impatiens, creeping Charlie, snapdragon, alyssum, viola, artemesia, and godetia.

Music

Sound Quiz

Materials
Tape recorder
Blank cassette tape

Directions
Go around your house, yard, school, and neighborhood listening for interesting sounds. Tape sounds, leaving about ten seconds of blank tape between sounds. Make sure you make a list

on paper of the sounds in order. You should also say a number on the tape before each sound. Once the tape is finished, let friends and family take the sound quiz. Keep a record of how many correct answers each person gets and announce the winner after everyone has taken the quiz.

Sound Effects

Materials
Real or handmade instruments
Anything that makes a sound

Directions
Use your instruments or sound makers to create sound effects for a story, play, or any scene you imagine. Here are a few examples:

- Water scene—the idea is to imitate the sounds of water running, splashing, dripping, or bubbling. Maybe you are at the sea or by a river or lake.
- A machine—most machines move with a rhythmic quality. Find clickers, clackers, drums, and cymbals to create interweaving rhythms. Make the machine run at different speeds, have a part break down, or try to start the machine up.
- Ghost stories—try using clock chimes or soft trembling notes that have no real rhythm.
- A thunderstorm—start with a crash of thunder with cymbals, drums, or pans, then a sprinkling of rain which could be fingertips pattering on a wood tabletop or a faucet dripping on a lid.

Think of other scenes you might create!

Music Appreciation

Materials
Tapes or CDs of various pieces

Directions
It is difficult to know where to begin when you want to learn something about classical music. The best way to learn about music is to listen to it. Start with some popular classical pieces. Most libraries have the following well-known pieces available on tape or CD:

- Mozart's Piano Concertos, numbers 20-27
- Beethoven's Fifth Symphony
- *Carnival of the Animals*, by Saint-Saens
- Britten's *Young Person's Guide to the Orchestra*
- *Peter and the Wolf*, by Prokofiev

Listen to the selected piece at least five times. If you find a piece or a composer you love, write it down in a notebook with a few notes to remind you what the piece is like, then listen to other pieces by that composer. There are many books on composers' lives that are fun reading. Why not read about the composer while you are listening to the music?

One Man Band

Materials

Things that make noise found around the house: bells, beans, milk bottle tops, pan lids, bicycle horns, harmonica, spoons, chains, glass bottles, whistle, homemade drums, tambourine. See how creative you can be in the search.

Directions

The idea is for you to become the instrument. As you move around banging your knees together, wiggling your head, and shaking your feet, music will be made! Here are some ideas:

- Mouth—blow a harmonica, whistle, glass bottle, recorder, or kazoo.
- Neck—hang bells, use string to hang a drum, xylophone, or tambourine.
- Under the arm—a bike horn tied to your upper arm so when you press your arm to your side a honking sound is made.
- Waist—drum, xylophone, small pots, or metal objects tied together.
- Elbow and wrist—tie on small bells.
- Hands—shaking a rattle, playing drums.
- Knees—tie things to clash against each other like foil plates, cymbals, saucepan lids, or small tins filled with dried beans.
- Ankles—tie bells, jingles, or a rattle.

Mini Opera

Materials
Costumes
Props

Directions
An opera is a play set to music. There can be some spoken words as in an ordinary play, but in an opera, song is the main dialogue. Pick a play that everyone knows or write one of your own. Instead of speaking the lines, everyone must sing them!

Note: Ask your Mom or Dad if one evening you can all sing to each other instead of speaking.

Recorder

Materials
Recorder
Beginner book

Directions
A recorder is a plastic or wooden flute-like instrument that is very easy to learn. Recorders are inexpensive, can be taken anyplace you go, and are fun to play. You can buy one at your local music store. Be sure to get a beginner book that has songs you like and a chart showing which fingers play each note. Find a friend that plays the piano and play a song together.

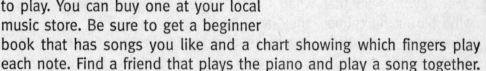

Wind Chimes

Materials
Round or square plastic or
strong cardboard lid
Nails of different sizes
String
Scissors

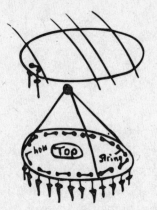

Directions
The idea is to mount the nails
close together so that when the
wind blows the chimes, they jan-
gle against each other. Tie a piece of string to the top of one nail. With
the tip of the scissors, poke a hole through the lid and pull the string
through the hole, then poke another hole and put the string back
through the lid to tie to another nail (see illustration). When all the nails
have been added, tie three or four pieces of string spaced evenly around
the edges of the lid and tie them together at the top to hang. Hang from
a tree branch, over a doorway, or anyplace the wind will hit them.

Rapping Rhythm

Directions

A rap song is fun to create. Here's how you do it: think of something you want to say, then write down the words in groups of rhymed couplets (a couplet is two lines of poetry about the same length). In rap, the voice is used like a drum. The rhymed words are spoken to a syncopated beat. That means the words that are emphasized must be off the usual beat. Here is an example:

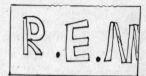

Syncopated- I want to GO far AWAY
A place where NO body SAYS
On the beat- I've GOT to GO
SomePLACE I KNOW
Listen to some rap music to get an idea how it's done.

Sing a Song

Directions

Everybody can sing. The more you do it the better you become. Pick any song you like, learn all the words to it and listen to the melody many times. Once you think you know the melody, experiment by putting your hand on your throat and humming to the song. Try it again, but this time say "ah" or "oh" where each word in the song would be.

Experiment making your voice loud and soft. Try making the song sound angry, sad, happy, or loving. Now sing along with the real words. Sing your song every day until you like the way it sounds, then learn a new one.

Poem Song

Materials
Book of poems

Directions
Find a poem you like. Read over it a few times, noticing the natural rhythm of the words. As you read the poem, let the melody develop in your mind. Hum along as you go over the words in your head. It is fun to come up with a tune to go along with the words.

Develop a tune and sing the words to that tune. When you finish the first poem try another. You may want to add a drum or tambourine to keep the beat.

Concert Time

Directions

Have you ever been to a concert? There are different kinds of music played at concerts: rock, jazz, folk, and classical. There are concerts that feature one, two, or three instruments as well as entire orchestras and singing groups. Many concerts are free. Look in the paper to find out where and when they are. Ask your school music teacher if she knows of any upcoming concerts you might like to attend. Once you pick a concert to go to, do some research on the style of music you will hear. If possible, go to the library and check out a CD or cassette tape and listen to it. Music always sounds more interesting once you have listened to it a few times.

Rain Maker

Materials
Wooden box measuring one yard long
by 4 to 6 inches wide and 2 inches
high
50 two-inch nails
½ cup dried peas

Directions
Find someone who can help you make
the box. A lumber yard can cut the
wood to specific measurements so all
you have to do is glue or nail it together. If you cannot make a whole
box, simply hammer the nails into a single piece of wood and place it
inside a cardboard box (from a florist), then tape the box shut. If you
are using a wooden box, hammer the nails in a random pattern (see
illustration) into the long piece of wood. Attach the sides with small
nails. Put the handful of peas into the box and nail the lid in place.
Paint or decorate the outside if you like. Hold the rain maker vertically
and listen to the peas sift through the nails sounding like rain. Then flip
the rain maker the other way vertically. Listen to by itself, play along
with music, use it for sound effects while acting, or if you ever miss a
rainy day.

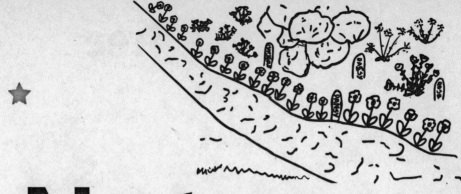

Nature

Plant a Tree

Materials
Tree seedling

Directions
Plant a tree in your yard, watch it grow and change, sit by it and talk about your problems, nurture and love it! Here's how you do it. Dig a hole bigger than the seedlings roots. Pour water into the hole to give your tree an extra drink on its first day. Set the tree in the hole and cover its roots with soil, filling the hole and packing the dirt around it as you go. Put wood chips, bark, and leaves around the base of the tree, but not right next to the trunk. The leaves and bark will break down and provide food for the tree. This is called mulching. Water the tree regularly the first few weeks.

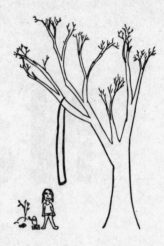

Note: Plant your tree on a special occasion like the first day of school, a birthday, the day you move into a new house, when a baby brother or sister is born, etc.

In the Wild

Directions

Have you ever wondered how plants grow in the wild when nobody plants them or waters them? Do an experiment in your backyard. Find a bit of dirt and ask if it can be yours. Now just leave it alone and watch what grows. The spot will go to seed which means  "weeds" will grow. However, most so-called "weeds" are really wild flowers that birds and other creatures love to feed on. If you like your wild spot and want to keep it as part of the garden, cut down the plants to about six inches off the ground. Do this in late fall after the flowers have bloomed. You have given something very special back to nature, a place for her to be herself!

Backyard Friends

Directions

Even if you have a very small backyard, chances are small animals live there. Animals that live close to humans are squirrels, raccoons, rabbits, mice, skunks, and birds. Investigate your yard by looking for nests, holes in the ground, tracks on the ground, or garbage taken out of the bin. Write down your observations on

an old brown paper sack. Draw a picture of each animal you might see. Whenever you see that animal, make a mark next to the picture on the bag. Roll up your bag and tie with a string. Keep it handy for any new spotting.

Garden Tour

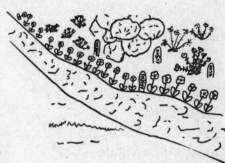

Materials
Wooden popsicle sticks or tongue depressor sticks (at a craft store)
Permanent paint pen

Directions
If you are lucky enough to have plants around your home, see if you can discover what they are called. Your parents might know or you could get a book from the library that has lots of pictures. Matching your plant to a picture is easier to do when there are flowers on the plants since plain leaves are harder to identify. Once you know the name of the plant, write it on a wooden stick with a permanent paint pen. Stick it in the ground next to the plant. When friends and relatives come to visit give them a garden tour. You will be proud to sound like a professional gardener!

City Birdbath

Materials
Wooden window box
Flower seed or plants: zinnia,
verbena, marigolds
Potting soil
Plastic container small enough
to fit in the window box

Directions
If you live in the city or you want
to see birds at your window, try a window box with a bird bath as the
main attraction. Plant your selected seed or plants in soil in the window
box, leaving room for the plastic container to fit in the middle. Fill the
pan with water and place in the window box. If the water is over two
inches deep, place a rock in the middle for birds to perch on. Rainwater
is best, so whenever you can, collect it and save it to use when refill-
ing the bird bath. You might want to string popcorn, berries, raisins, or
nuts around the edge to draw the birds' attention.

Camp Out

Materials
Tent or large sheet with plastic
ground cover
Blanket or sleeping bag
Pillow
Flashlight

Directions
Are you bored sleeping in your bed-
room every night? Pick a warm weekend night and ask if you can pitch a
tent in the backyard. If you don't have a tent, throw a large sheet over
the clothesline, stake it into the ground with sticks, then put a plastic
ground cover or pool floating mattress on the grass under the sheet.
Ask a friend to join you. The best way to experience nature is simply to
be outside, listen, feel, and appreciate.

Tree Feeder

Materials
Berries, seeds, raisins, apples
Popped popcorn
String
Fabric strips
Needle
Thread

Directions
Find a tree about your size in your yard (Christmas type trees work well). String the popcorn, berries, seeds, raisins, and apple pieces onto a thread. This is done by threading a needle with a two-foot long thread, tying a knot at the bottom, then putting the needle through the foods one at a time. The two-foot-long threads can be tied together once they have the food on them. Go out to the tree and loop the food thread around the branches. Many birds will be attracted to your feeder tree. In springtime, hang colored string, fabric pieces, and yarns on the tree and watch the birds snatch them up to build their nests. You may even be able to walk around the neighborhood and spot your thread in nests!

Note: Other things to hang on your tree include: a pine cone smeared with peanut butter, half an orange, a string of whole unshelled peanuts.

Bug Hunting

Materials
Clear container
Netting or waxed paper
Rubber band
Spoon
Overripe banana
Brown sugar
Magnifying glass

Directions
Have you ever taken the time to observe bugs? They are amazing creatures. They fly, buzz, sting, leap, and even light up. A good way to attract bugs is to put out something sweet like a banana with brown sugar sprinkled on top. Let the banana mixture sit outside a while, then spread it onto the bark of a tree. Check it regularly to see what new bugs you have attracted. Look through the magnifying glass and draw what you see. Come out at night with a flashlight and see if there are any newcomers. If you want to watch a particular bug, put it in your container with a bottle cap of water, a stick, and some green leaves. Cover the container with netting or waxed paper (make sure to poke small holes). Return your bug to the place you found him within twenty-four hours.

Worm Farm

Materials
2 old buckets
Dirt
Garden worms
1 cup dry-meal dog food

Directions
If you like to fish or live near a lake, a worm farm could be a fun hobby! To prepare the bucket, make plenty of small drainage holes on the sides and bottoms with a hammer and a thin nail. Fill the buckets with rich garden soil, add the dog food, and mix well. Sprinkle water on the soil until it is moist but not soggy. Now go digging in your yard or compost pile to find twenty-five worms. Put them on top of the soil filled buckets and watch them burrow out of sight. Stand the bucket on bricks in a pan full of water to keep the ants from eating the worms. Start a crop of worms in the second bucket after a month to give you a steady supply. Check your worm farm once a week to see if it is still moist. Too much water is worse than too little. Every three weeks, dump the top five inches of dirt out and mix it with a half cup of dog food. Dump the rest of the dirt out, put the dirt with the dog food in the bottom of the bucket, and pile the rest of the dirt back in. This is a good time to check how your farm is growing. You should have hundreds of worms in twelve weeks.

Garden Restaurant

Materials
Plant seedlings that grow in your area that animals and birds like to eat
Spoon
Jar or pitcher

Directions
If you would like to watch wild animals in your own garden, simply plant what they like to eat. Rabbits love clover, birds like berries, and squirrels like acorns. Your local nursery or plant store could tell you what animals in your area like to eat, or you might ask a neighbor or parent that gardens. When you find out what the animals like to eat, you can buy the seeds or a small plant. You might even be able to take one in the wild and grow it yourself. If you are planting seeds, follow the instructions on the packet. If you are planting a seedling, dig a hole with a spoon a bit bigger than the plant's root, put some water in, then delicately place the plant in the hole and fill it with dirt, packing as you go. Water your new garden regularly and look forward to meeting your new animal friends when your plants grow and produce nuts, fruit, and greenery.

Lake View in a Dish

Materials
Old dish
Green sand (from pet shop)
Stones
Shiny blue cellophane paper
Silver foil
Moss, twigs, leaves

Directions
Go outside and collect some materials like moss, pieces of pine tree branches, twigs, leaves, and stones from your yard or park. Lay the silver foil on the base of the dish or plate. Place the blue cellophane on top of the foil and sprinkle the green sand around the lake. Then place the rocks and other items you collected where you desire. Set your created lake on a shelf and when you are bored look at it and imagine what it would be like to be playing by a lake.

Waterslide

Materials
Large plastic sheet, 12 feet or longer
(hardware store)
Hose with a sprinkler
Grass to put slide on

Directions
Water is one of nature's biggest gifts—play with it today! Spread the piece of plastic out on a flat piece of grass, making sure to give yourself running room. Use smooth rocks, buckets filled with water, or tent spikes pushed all the way into the ground to hold the plastic down. Now set the sprinkler so it continuously wets the plastic sheet. To use the slide, take a running start, then slide down on your stomach, back, or feet. Make sure to go one at a time so you don't crash. After a while you may want to move the slide to another location on the grass.

Note: Thin plastic will work, but will tear easily. It is better to buy a thicker tarp off the roll at a hardware or building supply store and have it for a few summers.

Build a Terrarium

Materials

A clear glass container with a wide neck to allow your hand in
Small stones or gravel
Activated charcoal (get from pet store)
Potting soil
Small sponge
Piece of screen, mesh, or cheesecloth
Plants or moss

Directions

A terrarium is a completely self-supporting "ecosystem." The plant life replenishes the air with oxygen, light shining through provides the light and power source, and water comes from the moisture in the soil. As the dead leaves fall off, they decompose providing food for the soil. How to make one:

1. Select your plants. They should be small, like shade, and not grow too fast or too tall.
2. Put gravel on terrarium floor.
3. Sprinkle a small amount of activated charcoal on top.
4. Cover with a piece of screen with a slit cut in the middle
5. Slice the sponge to one third inch wide and stick it in like a candle between the slit in the screen and anchor it in the gravel. The sponge will bring moisture up to the plant roots.
6. Cover with potting soil.
7. Gently make small holes and place plants in them, packing the soil loosely around them.
8. Spritz your plants with water and cover. Add small figures.

Your terrarium may look a little limp for a few days but will get used to its new environment in no time.

Sundial

Materials
12 inch by 12 inch piece of heavy
card stock
Block of wood
Thumb tacks

Directions
An old way to tell the time was to use
the sun and the shadows it cast. You
can make a sundial to put in your back-
yard that will tell you what time it is. First, take the heavy card stock and
fold it corner to corner, then cut the card in half. Fold a flap on the bottom of the card to tack into the piece of wood. Attach the card to the
wooden block, making sure the triangle is straight up and down. Place
the sundial on a flat surface in the sun. Every hour, mark off where the
shadow is cast. You might even want to paint a nature design on the
wood block. Remember to keep the sundial facing the same direction so
your hour marks will be accurate.

Snail Farm

Materials
Clear plastic bottle
Bean bag or play dough
Soil
Lettuce or weeds
Snails from the garden

Directions
Your snail farm will be contained within the plastic bottle. Cut a small door in the side of the bottle about three inches by two inches so that when the bottle is on its side the door is at the top. Next, place damp soil in the bottle. Go outside and look for snails in the yard. Look around leafy plants, in the vegetable garden, or at the base of brick walls. Put them in your snail farm and give them fresh food like lettuce and weeds. Seal the door at the top with some clear tape and punch holes in the tape for air vents. Make sure the bottle top is sealed. Watch your snails for a few days then let them go.

Note: Snail facts: Snails have 25,000 teeth. They slide on their belly which is called a foot. They leave a slimy trail behind which helps them slide without hurting themselves. That fluid can also be used to seal the shell so the snail can live up to three years without food or water.

Number Magic

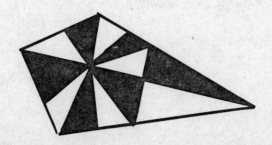

How Much Is Your Name Worth?

Materials
Pencil
Paper

Directions
Write your full name on a piece of paper. Write the alphabet from A to Z and number the letters 1 to 26. Let each number equal one dollar. Now calculate the value of your name.

Here is an example: Jonathan Gray.
J=$10, O=$15, N=$14, A=$1, T=$20, H=$8, A=$1, N=$14, G=$7, R=$18, A=$1, Y=$25. The total = $134!
Try this number game with your friends and family.

Fish Math

Materials
Pencil
Paper

Directions
Draw a fish on the piece of paper. Copy this number puzzle under the fish. Cover the Note below because that's where the solution is. Now see if you can solve this number puzzle.

"How much does a fish weigh if its tail weighs 4 kilograms, its head weighs as much as its tail and half its body and its body weighs as much as its head and tail together?"

Answer: 32 kilograms.

Count Off

Materials
Pencil
Paper

Directions
Draw a circle on the piece of paper. Copy this number puzzle underneath. Cover the Note below because that's where the answer is.

"Mr. Ara Besk is teaching a dance class.
He has his students space themselves evenly around a circle and count off. Student number 16 is directly opposite student number 47. How many students are in Mr. Besk's class?"

Answer: 62 students

Who Am I?

Materials
Pencil
Paper

Directions
"I am a two-digit number. The sum of my digits is 11. If my digits are reversed, I will be 45 less than who I am. Who am I?"

Answer: 83

The Perfect Square

Materials
Paper
Pencil

Directions
Draw several squares on the piece of paper. Write this number problem on the piece of paper also. Cover the Note below because that's where the answer is.

"Which integers from 1 to 100 have the sum of their digits equal to a perfect square?" Can you find 20?

Answer: 1, 4, 9, 13, 18, 22, 27, 31, 36, 40, 45, 54, 63, 72, 79, 81, 88, 90, 97, 100

Phone Tree

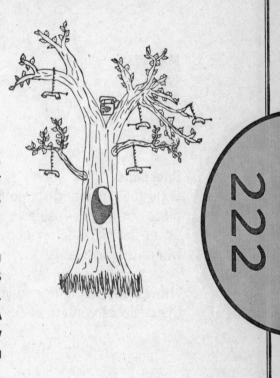

Materials
Pencil
Paper

Directions
Draw a tree with many branches. Write this number problem on the piece of paper also. Cover the Note below because that's where the answer is.

"Your school has a telephone tree to inform students and teachers when school is closed due to snow or other interruption. Each person will call two other people. A phone call takes two minutes. After thirty minutes, how many people will have been called?"

Answer: 987

Circus Ring

223

Materials
Compass
Ruler
Paper
Pencil

Directions
Copy the circle and six points onto a piece of paper using a compass. Cover the Note below because that's where the answer is.

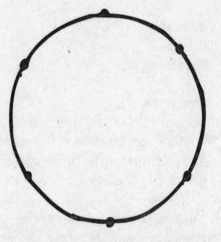

"How many triangles can you draw using any three of the six points on the circle as corners of the triangle?"

Answer: 20

Magic Square

Materials
Paper
Pencil
Ruler

Directions
Copy this diagram onto the piece of paper. Cover the Note below because that's where the answer is.

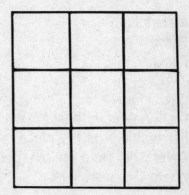

"Place the numbers 1 through 9 in the squares of the diagram so that no two rows, columns, or diagonals add up to the same number."

224

Answer: Top row: 5, 2, 7, Middle row: 1, 6, 8, Bottom row: 4, 3, 9

How Many Eggs in the Basket?

Materials
Pencil
Paper

Directions
Draw an empty basket. Write this number problem on the piece of paper also. Cover the Note below because that's where the answer is.

"If the eggs in the basket are counted by 2's, 3's, or 5's, there is one egg left over each time. What is the smallest number of eggs that could be in the basket?" When you have found the answer, fill your basket with eggs.

225

Answer: 31

Kite Triangles

Materials
Pencil
Paper
Ruler

Directions
Draw the kite diagram on the piece of paper. Cover the Note below because that's where the answer is.

"How many triangles can you count in your diagram?"

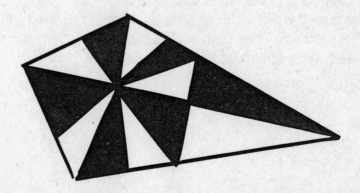

Answer: 28

Library Run

Materials
Pencil
Paper

Directions
Draw the problem on the piece of paper. Cover the Note below because that's where the answer is.

"Morgan and Troy are running from home to the library. Troy runs half the distance and walks half the distance. Morgan runs half the time and walks half the time. They both run at the same speed and walk at the same speed. Who arrives at the library first?"

Answer: Morgan: Because she spends more time running she finishes first.

5's

Materials
Pencil
Paper

Directions
Write the numbers from 1 to 100 on the piece of paper. Cover the Note below because that's where the answer is.

"If you wrote all the whole numbers from 1 to 100, how many times would you write the digit 5?"

Answer: 20

Parties

Bike Photo Safari

Materials
Bikes
Disposable cameras

Directions
This party is a picture hunt on bicycles. Each team of two or three kids gets a safari clues list. The team must use the clue list and photograph the location they believe is correct within a determined time limit. When everyone

returns, someone takes the photos to a one-hour photo shop (you may be able to prearrange this so you can get them in less than an hour). The party continues with lunch or dinner. When the photos are returned, display them on the wall. Photographs of correct locations will be judged for artistic quality as well as accuracy. Award prizes in many different categories: most artistic, picture furthest off the clue list, most locations correct, etc.

Note: Make sure everyone participating has a bike helmet and understands bicycle safety rules.

Scavenger Hunt

Directions

The idea of a scavenger hunt is to find all the items on a list and return them to a designated place as quickly as possible. There are many ways to organize a hunt and many choices to make. You can play as individuals or on teams either inside the house or outside. Here are a few ideas to try:

- All items on the list are easily found in the backyard (they can be hidden before the party). Things like a red leaf, matchstick, old bottle or can, feather, etc.
- Each person or team is given a different list of items to find by asking people around the neighborhood.
- Alphabet hunt—must find something for each letter of the alphabet.
- Indoor hunt where each person looks for things and checks them off their list when they find them without picking them up.
- Newspaper hunt—each person is given a list of words, sentences, advertisements, or photographs that are to be cut out or circled in a newspaper.

River Rafting

Materials

Plastic bottles with screw lids—
you need at least 100, so contact
a recycling center or have everyone you know save them for you
Large onion bags—16 bags to
make a raft for two people
Plastic fishing line
Needle

Directions

Pick a location that has a stream, creek, or river. Ask everyone to bring
a picnic lunch. You can supply the lemonade. Send invitations at least
two weeks before the party so everyone has time to collect plastic bottles and onion bags. How many bottles and bags you get will determine
the size and shape of the raft. To make the raft, put one onion bag
inside another for extra strength, then fill it with plastic bottles making
sure all the lids are fastened tightly so no water gets in. Use the fishing line and a large needle to sew up the openings in the bags. When
you have all the bags stuffed, sew them together. When it's time to try
out the raft, make sure the people riding it are wearing life jackets.

Cardboard Cake Surprise

Materials
2 cardboard boxes (both must be large enough to cover you, one bigger for the bottom layer and a smaller one for the top)
Brown paper and tape (use grocery bags)
Scissors
Paint, crayons, markers

Directions
Have you ever thought it would be fun to pop out of the cake at a party and surprise everyone? Here's how you make the cake. Cut a square about two inches from the edge in the small box. Cut off the top flaps if there are any. Cut a hole the same size in the larger box. Tape the two boxes firmly together. Cover the hole in the small box with brown paper. Decorate the cake with paint, paper cut-outs, fringes, Styrofoam, or anything you want. Make sure you climb into position before everyone sits down at the table. When it's least expected, rip through the brown paper and yell, "Surprise!"

Note: This would be a good trick if someone is coming to the party that nobody knows is in town.

Ghost Story Party

Materials
Old pair of tights
Rubber glove
Sand
Flour
Peeled grape
Dried apricot
Banana peel
Cooked noodles
Balloon

Directions

The above materials will be used to make body parts that will be passed around while the stories are being told. Cut one leg off the tights, fill it with sand, then tie off the top. Fill the rubber glove with flour and tie at the bottom. Cook the noodles, drain them, and put them in a bowl for brains. Fill the balloon with water for the head. The dried apricot is an ear, the banana peel rubbed with oil is a tongue, and the peeled grape is an eye ball. Make sure you collect a large selection of ghost stories before your party. You might be able to recruit an adult to read or tell the stories so you can listen. Other ideas for the party might include making a haunted house, walking through a graveyard, or making monster masks.

Crazy Cooks Party

Directions

The main activity at this party is cooking. Pick a menu all the ingredients. Set up the ingredients at different work stations and let kids work in groups to prepare the recipe. An adult should stand by to answer questions and monitor cooking. Decorate the table by tying balloons to pots and pans. Put chips, popcorn, and snacks into kitchen containers like blenders and pots. Give cloth aprons away as party favors. You could even supply fabric paint and let everyone decorate their own apron.

First Formal

Directions

Send formal invitations to about ten children. They should resemble wedding invitations with full names and addresses written out. Decorate the party area with real or artificial flowers, tall candles, white tablecloths, and name cards. Pick up the children with a chauffeur service (you can also get other parents or friends to volunteer). Upon arrival, have someone announce the name of the guest and blow a horn or beat a drum. Have appetizers brought around on trays before dinner as the children mingle. After dinner, play music for dancing (square dancing is fun or have someone teach the waltz).

Decoration ideas: Tape white butcher paper to the table top and make a design with crayons or paint to match the flowers. Make name cards out of plain index cards by folding them in half so they stand like tents.

Olympic Games

Materials
Each child brings a prize, wrapped up (used or new), which is then put in a big bag upon arrival.
Big container of lemonade or water

Directions
Make a list of all the events you can remember from the Olympic games. Include other events that might be special to your neighborhood like grass rolling, acorn picking, leaf catching, or creek walking. Make sure the events are safe and appropriate for the ages of children involved. Here are some things you might include: running races, swimming races, softball throw, long jump, Frisbee throw, tennis tournament, basketball toss, etc. If you don't have room in your yard, meet at a park that might have a swimming pool, basketball court, or other extras. The winner of each event picks a prize from the gift bag.

Beauty Shop

Directions

Create a beauty salon for your child! Get some grown-ups or baby-sitters to do the following jobs: nails, hair styles, foot or hand massage, facials, makeup application, and serving food. The girls move from station to station. While they are waiting,  the girls can chat as they look at magazines. Have someone serving lemonade and chocolate covered strawberries. Get a group picture of everyone at the end!

Party gift idea: Scented bath salts. You will need Epsom salts and glycerin (both bought at pharmacy), food coloring, cologne, perfume, rosewater or essential oils, a jar, ribbon, fabric or lace, liquid soap. To make, add one tablespoon glycerin, two to four drops of food coloring, and the fragrance. Stir. Pour the fragrant colored glycerin into a bowl and add the salts. Stir gently with your fingertips. Put in a decorated jar.

Surprise, Surprise

Directions

This is a surprise party for the guests as well as the birthday person! Arrange the party for a weekend evening and tell all the kids' parents about the party, but not the children. The real party is a sleepover, so the parents will need to bring a sleeping bag over in advance. Ask parents to have their children in their pajamas at a certain time. The host drives to all the children's houses and picks them up. When they arrive at the house, knock on the door and yell "Surprise!"

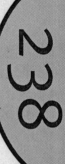
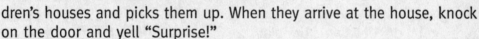

Fast Food Round Robin

Directions

Plan a meal to begin at one restaurant for an appetizer, perhaps a salad at Wendy's. The party continues at McDonald's for sandwiches and French fries. Then have dessert at an ice cream shop. Call restaurant managers ahead to reserve seating and arrange for party favors which are often available. Follow the meal with a game of miniature golf or bowling, or play games at a nearby park.

Oh, It's Your Birthday Party

Directions
Have you ever had a friend tell you that today is their birthday, and you know there is no party planned? Try this party to bring smiles to everyone. Telephone some friends to come over and ask them to bring anything they have around the house to decorate the party area. Ask each guest to cut out of a magazine or paper a gift they would have gotten the guest of honor. Make a box cake or make a big cookie, or if you are really pushed for time just serve ice cream in bowls. If you have a candle around the house, light it as you sing Happy Birthday. The most important thing about birthdays is remembering the day and feeling special. You can be assured that the guest of honor will always remember this party.

Note: This would also be a good way to celebrate a special event for someone in your family who comes home with especially good news.

Star Search

Directions

Send invitations to your friends two weeks in advance so everyone will have a chance to prepare an act either alone or with a few other people. Acts could be anything they like to do. They could be funny or serious and do not have to be professional since the idea is to have fun. The day of the party, clear an area in your yard or house for the stage. Get a few parents to act as judges giving out awards like best performance, most original, best actor or actress, funniest, silliest, one that you never want to see again, best imitation, best costume, etc.

Note: If you have video camera, tape the acts and play them back on the TV.

Puzzles

Tangrams

Materials
Poster board
Tracing paper
Colored felt tip pen
Scissors

Directions
Trace the tangram diagram on this page and reproduce it on the poster board. Color both sides with the felt tip pen and don't worry about going over the edges. Cut out the tangram pieces. There will be seven shapes altogether.

Can you put the pieces back into the square shape? Can you make a rectangle? What other shapes can you make?

Note: There are paperback tangram books available with hundreds of shapes to copy. Visit your public library and ask for the tangram books.

Rebus-Making

Materials
Paper
Pencil
Colored pens

Directions
You can create a letter or story using pictures and symbols instead of words. This is called a REBUS.

Here are some examples:
–instead of "I," draw an eye
–instead of "can," draw a watering can
–instead of "love," draw a heart
–instead of "be," draw a bee

Now try it on your own. Color your pictures and show it to a friend or parent to decipher.

Note: "Rebus" comes from a Latin word meaning "things." In the old days, signs and posters advertising carnivals were painted with pictures and no words to show people what "things" were going on.

Sentence Puzzle

Directions
See if you can solve this puzzle. Cover the Note at the bottom of the page because that's where the answer is!

There is three errers in this sentence.

What are they?

244

Answer: "Is" should be "are," "errers" should be "errors." The third error is that there are only two errors!

Magic Cards

Materials
Playing cards (optional)

Directions
Three playing cards are placed in a row as follows: the spade is to the right of the heart and diamond; the 2 is to the left of the heart; the 9 is to the right of the 5. Name the cards and their order from left to right.

Answer: 2 of diamonds, 5 of hearts, 9 of spades.

Flags

Materials
Paper
Pencil (preferably colored)

Directions
Make a perfect square on the sheet of paper. Using a ruler, divide it into eight equal parts as shown in the diagram.

How many different ways can you color half the area with a single color?

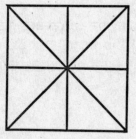

Answer: 13

Family Photo

Directions

A girl is looking at a family photo with her father. She points to a man in the photo and says to her father, "That man's mother was my mother's mother-in-law." What relation is the girl to the man in the photo?

Answer: His daughter

Matchstick Puzzle

Materials
16 match sticks

Directions
This figure has been made with sixteen match sticks. On a flat surface, make the same design with your match sticks—five squares altogether.

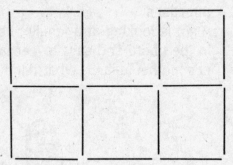

Can you move only three of the match sticks to form four squares?
The four squares must be the same size. (Cover the solution below while you try the puzzle.)

Answer: Remove the two match sticks on the lower left corner. Remove the lower right vertical match stick. Make a square with these three matches under the spare match sticks on the lower right.

What Day Is It?

249

Directions

When the day after tomorrow is yesterday, today will be as far from Sunday as today was from Sunday when the day before yesterday was tomorrow. What day is it now?

(Cover the solution below while you try the puzzle.)

Answer: Sunday

Birds

Directions
A large six-sided cage had a bird in each corner, five birds before each bird, and a bird on every bird's tail. How many birds were there in the cage?

(Cover the solution below while you try the puzzle.)

Answer: 6

A Box of Dots

Materials
Paper
Pencil

Directions
Copy this arrangement of dots onto the piece of paper—nine dots in three rows of three.

Can you join them all with four pencil strokes without lifting the pencil off the paper?
(Cover the solution below while you try the puzzle.)

Answer: Start at the upper right dot and draw a diagonal line to the lowest left dot. Go straight up to one inch beyond the upper left-hand corner dot. Draw a diagonal line downward through the top middle dot and the middle dot on the right-hand side and stop down on the base line. Now draw a line to your left through the remaining two dots back to where you started.

Hand Puzzle

Directions
Can you put your left hand where your right hand cannot reach it?
(Cover the solution below while you try the puzzle.)

Answer: Place it on your right elbow!

Tennis Anyone?

Directions

Two girls, Wesley and Brooke, and two boys, Troy and Rhett, love sports. One is a swimmer, one is a skater, one is a gymnast, and the other is a tennis player. One day they were seated around a square table.

The swimmer sat on Wesley's left.
The gymnast sat across from Troy.
Brooke and Rhett sat next to each other. A girl sat on the skater's left.
Who is the tennis player?
(Cover the solution below while you try the puzzle.)

Answer: Wesley is the tennis player.

Reading

Robust
Dogmatic · Dmosis
Bound · Chaos
Hemisphery · Hybrid
Abyss
Saber · Hexa...

Favorite Characters

Materials
Favorite reading books
Art supplies

Directions
Choose some favorite characters from books you have read. Take one character at a time and write down everything you know about him or her. Include such things as  birth date, friends, appearance, achievements, etc. If it is a historical character, find out about the times in which he or she lived. Create an informational poster of each one with drawings, facts, and descriptions. You could make a "Wanted" poster instead and design it on the computer.

Note: Save your posters for help with book reports or reading projects.

Illustrate Your Favorite Book

Materials
Paper
Art materials

Directions
Remember those picture books you
read as a child? Have you ever read a
book with no pictures? Did you wish
there were some? Here is an opportunity to illustrate one of your favorite
books. Choose a book and open it to
refresh your memory about the story

and characters. Decide where illustrations would have been helpful.
Now create your own. Use paper and pencil and do a rough draft. Color
your illustration in with felt tip pens, paints, crayons, or colored pencils,
or you might like to line it in black ink. Allow the illustration to dry. Fold
it neatly and slip it inside the book at the right place. Next time you
read your favorite book, you will be in for a pleasant surprise!

Winter Reading Log

Materials
Small notebook
Pen or pencil

Directions
There is nothing better to do on a cold winter day than curl up somewhere warm with a good book. At the first day of winter, start your Winter Reading Log. Enter the date and the year, e.g.,  December 20th, Winter of 2005. List all the books you read during the winter months. Allow a few lines below each title to include the author's name, how you felt about the book, whether you'd recommend it to your friends, and if you own it or borrowed it. You might like to include the titles of other books by the same author. Keep your Winter Reading Log updated year after year.

Note: Winter Solstice is officially the first day of winter. It falls on about December 22 in the Northern Hemisphere and on about June 22 in the Southern Hemisphere.

Predict the Ending

Materials
New reading book
Paper
Pencil

Directions
Before you start your next book, try this activity. Read the information on the covers. Read the Preface, Dedication, and anything else in the front of the book before the first chapter. Now read the first few pages of the story. Put the book down. Take a few minutes to think about how the story might end. Take a sheet of paper and write the ending you have predicted. Use the characters' names if you want and add characters if necessary. Fold the paper and tuck it inside the back cover. Continue reading the book, and when you have finished, read your prediction. Were you close?

Building Vocabulary

Materials
Dictionary
Small notebook
Pencil
String or yarn

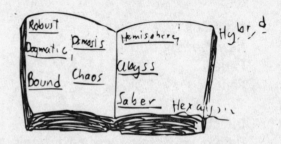

Directions
Most books that you read will have some words that are difficult to understand. They may be words that are very important to the story.

Buy a small notebook and attach a pencil to it with string or yarn. Have this notebook beside you while you read. When you come across a word that you don't know, write it down. If it is crucial to the story, look the word up in a dictionary right away and write down its meaning. If it can wait, continue reading after you have written the word down. Later (but not too much later), look up the new words in the dictionary and write down the meanings. Every once in a while, take out your reading vocabulary notebook and review all the new words you have learned. Share them with your parents or teacher.

Kids Book Club

Materials
Reading books

Directions
This reading activity is best done with a group of friends or other family members. You and the group should decide on a book you would all like to read. See if you can find enough copies of the book or take turns reading it. When everyone has finished the book, arrange an informal get-together. Before people come, ask each one to bring a question about the story. When you are all together, take turns sharing your individual questions with the rest of the group. When the discussion is over, talk about the next book you would all like to read...and start the process over again.

Story Board Game

Materials
Felt tip pens
Dice
Poster board
Index cards
Playing pieces
Yardstick

Directions
You can make your own game to illustrate the adventure in a story you have read. Draw the path the players will take on the poster board. Use the yardstick if necessary. Divide the path into squares (about one inch square) and decide which square will be the "start" and which one will be the "finish." Number the squares, leaving some as features of the story. The rest of the game is up to you. Make the rules simple and clear. The index cards can be used as "consequences" and "rewards" and should be placed in piles in the center of the board. When you are done, invite friends or family members to play the game with you.

Story Map

Materials
Paper
Colored pencils

Directions
Many of the books you read will involve interesting locations—an island, a neighborhood, a land far away, a journey. As you read the story, draw a map of where everything is. Add different features and landmarks as you continue reading. Label as much as you can and make your map

colorful. You might want to include a "key" so that the map will be easier to understand. It is very helpful to have a map if a story is complex. You can refer to it if you get lost.

Note: Check the map in Robert Louis Stevenson's *Treasure Island* and the maps in J. R. R. Tolkien's *Lord of the Rings*.

Reading Aloud

Materials
Book
Cassette tape recorder

Directions
Children should be encouraged to read aloud. They also like to listen while someone else reads to them. In order for oral reading to be a comfortable experience, it should be practiced before it is performed. Choose a short story or a part of a longer story that you would like to read aloud. Practice reading the paragraphs with the cassette tape recorder. Play back your reading and repeat recording until it sounds okay. This is particularly helpful if you have been asked to read in front of your class or to an audience. If you have had a chance to practice reading aloud, you will feel much more at ease when it is your turn to do it.

Note: Readers' Theater is another avenue for children who like to read aloud. Investigate if your school has a program or start a group with your friends.

Reading Webs

Materials
Paper
Pencil

Directions
Webbing is a way to show that you understand how the whole story is put together. You have probably done webbing at school in writing, science, and social studies. You can make reading webs just as well. Practice making a

reading web with a familiar story. Read it first and then pick out the key words. Things to consider are: the characters, the actions they perform, the places they visit, the objects they use, and the problems they run into. Write the names of the main characters on the paper. Add the other key words, joining them to each other with lines just the way they are connected in the story. Soon you will have the whole story in a web. This will enable you to see the ins and outs of the story all on one page. Next time, make a web of a brand new story.

Repairs

Bicycle Tire Repair

Materials
Tire repair kit
Bowl or pail of water

Directions
If you have punctured the inner tube of your bicycle, you can easily repair it yourself. Buy a bicycle  tube patch kit from a bicycle or hardware store. It contains adhesive, assorted patches, sandpaper, and instructions. Remove the inner tube by prying one edge of the rubber tire off the rim. To find the hole, pump some air into the tube and dip it into a bowl of water. You will see bubbles coming from the hole. Dry and clean the area around the hole. Carefully follow the instructions in the kit.

Note: Keep a tire repair kit and a pump on your bicycle somewhere. You never know when you might need them!

Patching

Materials
Fabric and matching thread
Needle
Dressmaker pins
Chalk
Tracing paper
Scissors

Directions
Lay the item to be patched flat. Using the chalk, mark off the area the patch should cover, allowing for a half-inch border. Place the tracing paper over the chalk markings and copy the shape. Pin the tracing paper on the fabric and cut out the patch. Remove the tracing paper. Turn under the half-inch border on the wrong side and iron flat. Pin the patch on the clothing right side up. Thread the needle, knot the end of the thread and sew the patch onto the clothing with a small slip stitch. If you have access to a sewing machine, sew a seam one-fourth of an inch from the edge of the patch.

Repairing Zippers

Directions

You may not need to replace a zipper that has come apart below the slider, especially if it is a metal one. Here's how you can rethread a broken zipper.

1. Pry off the end-stop at the bottom of the zipper and run the slider down to the tape ends below the lowest teeth.
2. Line up the tape ends and ease them into the slider and move the slider upwards. The teeth should then come together.
3. Sew the tapes together across the lowest two pairs of teeth. Thread a needle with double thread and work five or six stitches across the teeth and into the tapes at each side.

Note: If the zipper is difficult to move, rub a soft pencil up and down the teeth. You could also try talcum powder if the fabric is light colored.

Cleaning a Toaster

Materials
1-inch paintbrush
Soft cloth

Directions
Toasters work more efficiently if they are cleaned regularly. To clean out a toaster and prevent trouble and burnt smells, do the following:

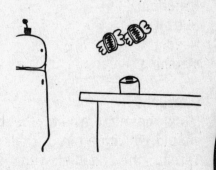

1. Disconnect the power cord.
2. Open the clean-out trap, usually at the base of the toaster.
3. Using the paintbrush, brush out crumbs. Never use a knife!
4. Blow crumbs and other food matter from parts you can't reach with the paintbrush.
5. Replace the clean-out trap.
6. Polish the outside with a soft cloth and connect the power cord.

Note: Cans of compressed air can be bought at a photography store. Use short bursts and do not aim the nozzle directly at the thin wire heating elements.

Sewing Buttons

Materials
Button
Needle
Matching thread

Directions
Mark the place where the button
should go with a pin or chalk mark.
Thread the needle with double
thread and knot the ends. Starting on the wrong side, sew the button
onto the fabric through the holes, about four to six times. Leave the
thread slack enough so the button will not be embedded in the fabric.
Finish by winding the thread around this thread shank before fastening
it off on the wrong side.

Note: Always sew buttons through two thicknesses of fabric. Buttons
that are subject to much strain should be supported by a small backing
button on the wrong side.

Repairing a Scratched CD

Materials
CD repair kit

Directions
You may not have to throw away that scratched compact disc. There are compact disc cleaning kits available at most music stores. Each kit contains a special super-fine abrasive material that polishes out deep scratches. The kit also includes a cleaning fluid that removes dirt, dust, and other particles from the surface of the disc. The kit allows you to clean and repair up to twenty-four discs.

Note: To find a store that sells the kit, go to the Yellow Pages of your phone book and look under "Records, Tapes, and Compact Discs—Retail."

Replacing a Lightbulb

Materials
New lightbulb
Soft cloth

Directions
If you are replacing the lightbulb in a flashlight, first make sure the batteries are not worn out. If you determine that only the bulb has failed, unscrew the metal ring that joins the head to the shaft (remember—right, tight; left, loose) and gently remove the top part of the flashlight. Unscrew the lightbulb and replace it with the new bulb. Screw the head and shaft back together again. If you need to replace a regular lightbulb in a reading lamp, for example, first disconnect the power cord. The bulb may be hot, so use the cloth to unscrew it from the base. Do not squeeze the glass bulb too hard. Screw in the new bulb and then connect the cord to the power source.

Note: Try using the energy-saver bulbs the next time you need to replace a worn-out bulb. They save you money in the long run.

Repairing a Cassette Tape

Materials
Splicing kit

Directions
If you have a broken or split cassette tape, you may not have to discard it. Buy a splicing kit at an audio equipment parts store. The kit contains a trimmer, splicing tape, and instructions on how to fix the tape if the broken ends are outside the cassette.

If the split ends are inside the cassette, you can do the following:
1. Cut off a strip of the sticky splicing tape in the kit.
2. Slide the strip inside the cassette to capture the ends of the broken tape.
3. Carefully fish the ends of the tape out of the cassette.
4. Make the splice according to the instructions in the kit.

Holes in the Wall

Materials
Spackling compound or putty
Spackling or putty knife or plastic ruler
Sandpaper (medium to fine)
Damp sponge

Directions
Wipe the area around the hole clean.
Soften the spackling compound or putty
and apply it to the hole with the knife.
Keep the handle of the knife as close to
the wall as you can, holding it on an angle. Smooth the compound so
that it blends with the surface of the wall around the hole as much as
possible. Allow it to dry, then reapply thinly. If it is a shallow hole,
smooth with a damp sponge. Allow to dry thoroughly. Finally, sand
smoothly and seamlessly with sandpaper.

Leaking Faucets

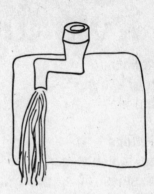

Materials
Washers
Steel wool
Toothbrush

Directions
Turn off the water before you start. The turn-off valve is usually below the sink or toilet fixture. The first area to check is the aerator. Unscrew the aerator from the nozzle. Using a toothbrush, remove any debris from the mesh of the aerator. Run water through it and tap gently so that there are no obstructions. Lightly clean the inside and outside with steel wool, but do not remove any metal. Replace the aerator. Turn the water back on and test it.

Another problem could be a worn-out washer. You should ask an adult to help you unscrew the handle and stem to get to the old washer. Pry it out with a screwdriver or pocket knife. Replace the washer with a new one of the same size. Put the faucet parts back together again, tightening slowly and carefully. Turn the water back on and test it.

Note: Many faucet parts are available in kits. These are most often listed under the trade name of the faucet and are available at hardware stores.

Removing Hard Food from the Microwave

Materials
Cup of water
Damp cloth

Directions
Food that has hardened on the floor and sides of a microwave oven is often difficult to remove. Do not use steel wool or abrasive cleaners to get the food off. Instead do the following:

1. Place cup of water in the oven. Turn the oven on full power for three minutes.
2. When the oven shuts off, keep the door closed for another five minutes to allow steam to soften the residue.
3. Open the door and let the steam escape. Do not stand too close.
4. Use the damp cloth to remove the soft spots.
5. If food still remains, repeat the procedure.

Buzzing Cordless Phones

Directions

Do you often get a loud buzzing sound when using a cordless phone? Here is what you can do:

1. Make sure no one in the house is using an electric appliance or electric tool.
2. Check to see if the battery is overcharged. If there is excess electricity, it will create interference. To fix this, leave the phone off the cradle until the battery discharges. Flip the switch to Off or Standby and replace the handset. Let the battery charge again.
3. If you suspect an amateur radio operator is operating nearby, you may want to return the phone to the dealer and ask to have the phone's frequency changed.

Replacing a Waistband Elastic

Materials
Safety pin
New elastic cord
Needle and thread

Directions
Remove the old elastic from the waistband of the garment (shorts, pajamas, or sweats) by carefully pulling it out. Measure the new elastic to fit your waist with a few inches to spare. Attach one end of the elastic to the  safety pin and close the pin. Pin the other end of the elastic to the fabric near the opening so that it doesn't disappear. Push the safety pin through the opening in the waistband with the elastic attached. Ease the safety pin all the way around the band until it comes out where it went in. Thread the needle and stitch the ends of the elastic together very securely. Tuck the stitched ends back inside the waistband and stitch the opening closed.

Room Decoration

"All About Me" Poster

Materials
Large piece poster board (any color)
Scissors
Glue stick
Glitter
Photographs
Magazines

All ABOUT ME

Directions
Look through photographs or magazines for things you like or that describe you. Cut them out and arrange them on the poster board. Make any design you like. Put pictures on that make you feel good, that express what you like and who you are. Hang on your wall with pride! Do one every six months and you will be amazed how much you will have changed.

Color Code Your Closet

Directions

Here's a fun and simple way to organize your room. Take all your clothes out of your closet and rearrange them by color. It also works well to organize them in groups like pants, shirts, jackets, dresses, etc. Enjoy being able to see and find everything!

Letter Door Sign

Materials
White and black paper
Colored pen
Metallic pen (optional)
White chalk

Directions
You are going to make a sign to hang on your door using the first letter of your name or your entire name. Be as creative as you can

designing your letter shapes. You may want to look at a calligraphy book for ideas. Draw your large letter on the white paper. Once you like the way your letter looks, cut it out and glue it onto the black paper. Using the colored pens, color the letters in. Use the metallic pen or a light color to outline the letter. Take the white chalk and make a decorative design on the black paper. If you really like the sign, glue it to a piece of plywood and paint over it with clear acrylic.

Four-Poster Bed

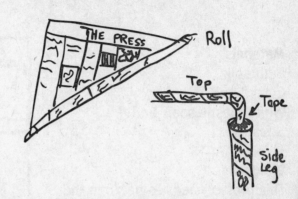

Materials
Lots of newspaper
Masking tape
Sheets
Fabric scraps
String or twine

Directions
Here's your chance to change your ordinary bed into one fit for a king or queen. You will need to make many strong newspaper tubes. To do this, roll at least six sheets of newspaper tightly starting at one corner. Tape the roll a few times to hold the roll together. Measure the height you would like the canopy to be. Join the newspaper rolls together with tape to make four legs as tall as you need. Tie them to the legs of your bed. If you have no legs on your bed, wrap the twine around the whole base of your bed a few times. Next, measure the distance between the legs for the top of the frame. Make the top frame a little longer than you need so the ends can be folded over and stuffed into the leg tops. Tape them securely. You can paint the newspaper if you want, but be careful not to drip paint on the bed or floor. Drape fabric scraps, sheets, ribbons, or anything you want to dress up the bed. Sweet dreams!

Spring Bulbs

Materials
Bulb soil
Crocus bulbs
White plastic soap bottle
Scissors

Directions
This project needs to be done the end of October and put away for four to six weeks. Cut the top from a plastic soap bottle, then cut as many holes in the side as you have bulbs. Fill the bottle with bulb soil and plant the bulbs so their necks peep out from the holes. Water over the sink since water will drain out the holes. Now keep the bottle in a cool, dark place for four to six weeks or until the shoots are about two inches long. Bring the bottle out into the light and water again. Continue to keep it moist and turn the bottle around occasionally so all the bulbs get light. The crocuses should flower around Christmas. When they finish flowering, cut off the dead stems and plant the bulbs outside in the garden to bloom next year.

Note: Check at your local plant store for other bulbs you can grow in your room at different times of the year.

Canvas Room Rug

Materials
Piece of plain canvas (the size
you want your rug)
Acrylic paint
Paintbrushes
Clear acrylic coating
Hot glue gun or sewing
machine

Directions
You may need someone to help you get the canvas rug ready to paint.
Fold the edges of the rug over a half inch and press with a hot iron.
Sew the edges with a sewing machine or use a hot glue gun. On a piece
of paper, work out the design for the rug. Use crayons to experiment
with color. When you are ready to begin, pencil the design onto the rug
and begin painting when it looks right. After the paint is dry, cover the
rug with a few coats of clear acrylic. Once the acrylic is dry, the rug can
be sponged clean with soap and water. Walk on your new rug with
pride.

Fabric Collage

Materials
Scissors, tweezers, liquid glue
3 dishes
Old paintbrush to spread glue
Scraps of fabric that match your room
colors or favorite team
Yarn, string, or ribbon
Something to do collage on, like an old
tabletop, bed headboard, frame, or just
a cardboard box
Liquid acrylic

Directions
With scissors, cut up the fabric into
small pieces and divide them into three dishes of pale, medium, and
dark tones. Draw the shape you will be filling in (tropical fish, parrots,
animals, and free designs work well). First, paint a small area with glue,
then put the fabric pieces on a little bit at a time. You may want to rub
over the top of the fabric with a piece of clean rag to make sure it is
flat. Use the yarn, string, or ribbon for added decoration. When your
project is completely dry you may wish to coat it with liquid acrylic.

Sponge Painting

Materials
Acrylic wall paint
Natural sponge

Directions
Before you begin sponge painting, move all the furniture to the center of the room and cover it with an old sheet. Wash the walls with a rag and a bucket of warm water with one tablespoon bleach added. Put the paint in a shallow pan, then dip one side of the sponge in and wipe it against the side of the pan. Start sponging at one of the corners by dabbing the sponge on the wall five to six times in a row, touching the edge of the last sponge mark with each dab. Sponge painting is supposed to look cloud-like and uneven. Use your imagination and be creative. It looks nice when a dark color is sponged on first (let dry) then a lighter coat added on top. Why not sponge the ceiling blue like the sky or do a design on one wall only.

Letter Holder

Materials
2 paper plates
Colored yarn
Crayons, paints, felt markers
Paper punch or sharp nail
Bobby pin

Directions
Cut one of the paper plates in half and leave the other one whole. Put the half plate on top of the whole plate with the tops of the plates facing each other. Punch holes through both plates big enough to thread yarn through. With the colored yarn and a bobby pin, stitch the two plates together. Decorate your letter holder in any way you like. Punch a hole at the top. With a six-inch length of yarn, make a loop for hanging the holder on the wall.

Border It Your Way

Materials
Drawn pictures or magazines
Scissors
Wallpaper paste
Old paintbrush

Directions
A border is a line of pictures pasted to the very top of the walls around the entire room. Collect pictures you draw or look through magazines you like for appropriate pictures. When you have enough pictures, mix up the wallpaper paste and brush it a little at a time where the border will be. Put one picture on at a time, gently rubbing over the picture with a clean cloth. If you get tired of this border, simply border over the top of it in the same way.

Snow Jar

Materials

1 jar with screw-top lid
Waterproof glue
Wallpaper paste
Glitter
Paints (oil-based)
Small toys, ornaments,
miniature trees

Directions

If you can't get to the snow in the wintertime, make some of your own. Take the jar lid and glue small toys, ornaments, trees, etc., to the lid. Make sure you don't use a water based glue. Paint the back of the jar white or black to create a background for the snow storm. You can also paint a scenic background if you want. Once the paint is dry, fill the jar almost to the top with water and sprinkle in about a teaspoon of wallpaper paste and some glitter. Stir the mixture and allow it to settle. Screw the lid back on and turn the jar upside down and give it a shake. Enjoy your instant winter scene.

Science

Egg Drop

Materials
Raw egg (and a few extra)
Packing materials
String or tape

Directions

The object of this activity is to wrap up an egg so that it won't break when dropped from a height. The recommended height is 12–15 feet. Design a container which will pro-tect the egg from breaking. It should be lightweight and sturdy. Most of all, it should withstand sudden impact with the ground.

Note: The Egg Drop is one of the events in the Science Olympics in which many schools participate. This could be your entry.

Paper Tower

Materials
Sheets of paper, 8 ½ x 11 inches
Paper clips

Directions
How high can you build a tower using only paper and paper clips? Your design should include a firm, broad base and some creative ways to make the tower as tall as possible.

Note: This activity can also be done with drinking straws and masking tape.

Tree Rings

Directions
In the spring, trees grow quickly and produce light-colored wood. In the summer, the tree grows more slowly and the wood is darker. The dark areas form rings. You can count the rings to find out how many summers old the tree is. Obtain a log of wood that has been sawed off crosswise and count!

Note: A tree grows in height or grows branches longer only at its tip.

Paper Airplane

Materials
Sheets of plain paper (recycled preferably)
Stopwatch or watch with a second hand

Directions
The object of this activity is to make a paper airplane and to see how long it can stay in the air. Try several shapes and designs and test them in an open space. Time the flight from the moment it leaves your hand until the moment it touches the floor or another object. What flight pattern tends to keep the airplane aloft? What tail design is most efficient?

Floating Needle

Materials
Water
Bowl
Newspaper
Sewing needle
Liquid detergent

Directions
Cut out a piece of newspaper about two inches square. Fill the bowl with water and float the newspaper on the surface of the water. Place the needle in the center of the newspaper. Carefully push the edges of the newspaper down into the water. As the newspaper gets wet and sinks, it will leave the needle floating. Now add a drop of liquid detergent to the water at the edge of the bowl. Notice how the needle quickly sinks to the bottom.

Note: Surface tension made it possible to float the needle on water. The needle was supported by the water. The detergent caused a break in the surface tension around the needle and it sank.

Balloon Rocket

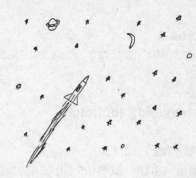

Materials
Balloon
Paper clips
Thin wire or string
Tape
Drinking straws

Directions
Hang the wire or string across the room. Make a rocket that will propel itself along the wire. Use the balloon to provide the rocket's power and the straw, paper clips and tape to guide it along the wire. Use your imagination and your knowledge of air power to make the balloon travel across the room. Remember, the air that is forced out of the balloon pushes the balloon along in the opposite direction.

Can you make a rocket system that will get across the room and then come back again?! Draw a diagram of your design.

Note: This science activity is based on Newton's Third Law of Motion— every action has an equal and opposite reaction.

Tornado in a Bottle

Materials
2 clear plastic large soda bottles
Tape
Water
Food coloring (optional)

Directions
Fill one of the bottles three-quarters full of water.
Add a couple drops of food coloring. Invert the
other bottle so that it sits on top of the first bottle with the openings together. Wind the tape
tightly around the necks of the bottles so that no
water can leak out. The top bottle should be securely balanced on top
of the bottom bottle. Now, hold the bottles with two hands and swirl
the water around. Turn upside down and watch what happens.

Note: Tornadoes can sometimes produce winds of 250 miles (400 km)
per hour. A water spout is a tornado over water and a dust devil is a
tornado over sand in the desert.

Bottled Egg

Materials
Egg, hardboiled and in its shell
Vinegar
Water
Milk bottle

Directions
Soak the egg in vinegar until the shell becomes soft. Lay the bottle on its side. Gently squeeze the soft egg through the neck of the bottle and let it slide to the bottom. Rinse the bottle with cold water to remove the smell of vinegar and to make the shell harden again. Now you can show this amazing achievement to your friends! (But don't tell them how you did it.)

Note: The egg shell is made of a chemical called calcium carbonate which dissolves when in contact with an acid, like vinegar.

Bouncing Raisins

Materials
6 raisins
Glass tumbler
Vinegar
Baking soda (or Alka Seltzer tablet)

Directions
Pour a cup of water into the glass jar. Add one teaspoon of baking soda and stir until dissolved. Gently add one-fourth cup of vinegar and wait until it stops fizzing. Drop in three or four raisins. Watch and see what happens (it takes about 10 to 15 minutes).

Note: The gas, carbon dioxide, that forms when you add vinegar to the baking soda forms bubbles all over the raisins. The raisins start to rise as the bubbles of carbon dioxide carry the raisins upwards and they fall when the bubbles are released.

How Does Rust Form?

Materials
Steel wool
Paper and pencil
Water
Shallow pan

Directions
Pour water into the pan until it is about one inch deep. Place the steel wool in the water. Make a chart with days one to five down the left side and the heading "What the steel wool looks like" on the right side of your paper. Each day, describe the appearance of the steel wool on your chart. Can you explain the changes?

Note: Iron is the main chemical in steel wool. In the presence of water, it "oxidizes" and forms iron oxide, or rust. That is why old cars rarely have rust in dry climates and often have rust in wet climates.

Kitchen Chemistry/Rock Candy

Materials
Clean 1 quart glass jar with wide mouth
Kite string
Paper clip
Pencil
Sugar
Boiling water

Directions
Fill the jar with sugar. Slowly pour the boiling water into the jar while stirring with a long-handled spoon until all the sugar is dissolved. Tie the paper clip to one end of the string and measure the height of the jar plus a few inches. Cut the string and tie the cut end to the pencil. Place the pencil across the mouth of the jar and roll the string around the pencil until the paper clip is just above the bottom of the jar. Place the jar on the kitchen window ledge. Rock candy crystals will grow on the string. The longer the string is in the jar, the larger the crystals will grow. From time to time, break up crystal formation on the jar and on the surface.

Note: Crystals form by precipitation from a hot solution that cools slowly or by evaporation of a liquid. Mineral crystals can also form in these two ways.

Effects of Acid Rain

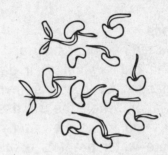

Materials
20 seeds
2 plastic bags
2 paper towels
Vinegar
Water

Directions
Fold the paper towels so that they fit inside the plastic bags. Moisten one towel with water and the other one with a dilute solution of vinegar and water. Count ten seeds and place them between the layers of towel. Slide the towels and seeds into the plastic bags. Label the bags "Water" and "Vinegar." Every two days, inspect your seeds and moisten the paper towels with the appropriate solution if they start to dry out. What do you notice after eight to ten days?

This experiment will show you the effects of acid rain on growing seeds. You may want to research the acid rain problem and start writing letters expressing your concerns.

Note: For more information about acid rain, write to:
The Acid Rain Foundation
1410 Varsity Drive
Raleigh, NC 27606

Cloud Expert

Directions

Did you ever wonder how and why clouds in the sky got their distinctive shapes? Air contains invisible water vapor. When the air rises, it becomes cooler and the water vapor turns into water droplets or it gets so cold that the water droplets freeze into ice crystals. These tiny droplets form the clouds you see when you look up into the sky. If the air is rising slowly, you will see thin streaks of cloud. When the air rises quickly, the clouds will appear puffy.

There are three main kinds of clouds which form at different heights in the air and are known by their different shapes:
1. Cirrus–have a feathery shape and are the highest.
2. Cumulus–have a fluffy shape (usually separated) and are at medium height.
3. Stratus–form in sheets and layers. These are lowest. Gray stratus means rain.

Find out more about clouds and how they are used to predict the weather.

Self-Esteem

My "Me" Scrapbook

Materials
Scrapbook
Scissors
Photos
Magazines
Paste or glue

Directions
The purpose of this activity is to start and maintain a personal scrapbook. It is ongoing, but does not have to be kept up daily. Start on the first blank page of your scrapbook and write your name, date of birth, address, and any other personal details. Thereafter, fill each page with pictures, photos, drawings, writings, and items that reflect who you are and who you want to be. Remember to include the date each time you find something you want to paste in. You can even include mementos such as tickets and postcards if they have personal significance. In the years to come, you will treasure this "me" book that you have made.

Note: Knowing who you are and what you want is fundamental to building positive self-esteem.

Family Rituals

Directions

Families are the building blocks of every culture and every family is different. Families tend to do the same kind of things together day after day and year after year. What are some of the things your family does together? Write a list and then make a poster. It would be a good idea to interview other family members, especially grandparents, to help you put together your family ritual list. You can illustrate your poster with photos of family events such as vacations, Thanksgiving dinner, and birthday parties. Place your family ritual poster where everyone can see it.

How to Relax

Directions

Relaxing is a way to reduce stress, but doesn't always come natural-ly. You can learn to relax. Here is a method that works with kids: Sit comfortably on the floor with legs crossed or lie down. Don't do this on your bed because you might fall asleep instead! Close your eyes and relax the muscles in your wrists, ankles, elbows, and knees.

Take some deep breaths and then breathe softly and evenly. Imagine you are smoothing out the skin on your forehead, cheeks, around your eyes, under your chin, and around your mouth. Relax your shoulders and feel your neck lengthen. Relax the muscles in your back. Let your tongue feel soft and open your lips slightly. Imagine you are floating on a soft cloud, weightless and peaceful.

When you feel ready to come back to earth, open your eyes and give yourself an overall stretch.

Homework Hints

Materials
Pencil and pen
Paper or notebook
Ruler, colored pens, eraser
Homework assignment

Directions
There's nothing better for boosting self-esteem than handing in homework that is on time and well-done. Here's how you can succeed at homework:

1. Write down the homework assignment in a special place, either on a homework assignment sheet or in a small homework notebook. Include the due date.
2. Take everything you need home with you, especially books and worksheets.
3. Find a quiet workspace at home where you won't be disturbed. It should be the same place every day. Keep extra pencils, paper, dictionary, ruler, eraser, computer disks, scissors, and all essential materials in this one place.
4. Take a short break from your homework every 20 minutes.
5. Ask an adult to check your work or help you review for tests.

Note: Read *Homework without Tears* by Lee Canter for further helpful suggestions.

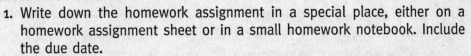

Writing About Feelings

Materials
Paper or diary
Pen or pencil

Directions
We all have many feelings and some of them can get in the way of our self-esteem. Learning to name what we feel means we can share those feelings with others and be more clear about what we want. Feelings often come in pairs; one is the opposite of the other. Can you name ten feelings and their opposites? For example, interested/bored, upset/relieved. Write them down. Write about a time when you felt these feelings. Try to find someone you can talk to about your feelings.

Start with your parents or a teacher or your school counselor. Remember that feelings aren't good or bad, right or wrong, they are emotions that you feel personally.

Fixing Mistakes

Directions

Nobody is perfect. We all make mistakes, but we don't always take responsibility for our mistakes. We blame someone else or pretend it didn't happen. The best way to deal with a mistake or poor decision is to fix it. An apology isn't enough—it doesn't repair the mistake. Fixing your mistake is called "restitution." For example, if you spill your glass of milk, don't expect someone else to clean up the mess. Fix it yourself. If your dog digs a hole in your neighbor's garden, offer to repair the damage by filling in the hole and replanting. This way, you take charge of the consequences for your mistakes.

Note: Read *Restitution* by Diane Chelsom Gossen.

What I Like about Me

Materials
Pencil
Paper

Directions
Basic to having high self-esteem is deciding you like who you are. We often wrongfully make that decision by looking in a mirror. Make five lists about what you like about yourself. Label the lists Appearance, Feelings, Abilities, Friendships, and Habits. Under each

label, list your strengths and positive qualities. For example, what do you like about your looks? What feelings do you have that you like? What are some things you do well? What do you bring to your friendships? What are your good habits at school and at home? Read these lists over when you are feeling down. Add to them from time to time with new discoveries about yourself.

Happiness List

Materials
Paper
Pencil

Directions
Sometimes we tend to remember the
bad things that happen to us more
than the good things. Write down five
things that happened yesterday. Read your list over. Did you remember
five good things, five bad things, or some of each? Whatever you wrote
down, you chose it to write down. You can practice remembering good
things and feelings and letting go of bad ones. Every day, write down
five things that happened which you felt good about. Write what happened and how you felt about it. The best time is before you go to bed
at night. These are your "happiness lists" and you can look them over
any time you are feeling down or unhappy. Your lists will help you do
more things that create happiness and will also help you collect and
store good feelings.

Power Play

Materials
Paper
Pencil

Directions
Having personal power in your life is not the same as having power over other people. You have personal power when you make decisions that affect your daily life, such as what you say, what you wear, what you eat, when you do your homework, who you play with, etc. There are some things that you don't have power over and other things that you would like to have power over.

Name five things that you have power over at home. Name five things you don't have power over at home. Name five things you would like to have power over at home. Choose one thing you would like to have power over. Talk it over with a parent and see if there are any options or compromises that everyone can live with.

Try the same exercise with school. Talk to a teacher, counselor, or administrator to see if you can make a change.

Note: For more ideas about how personal power affects self-esteem, read *Stick Up for Yourself* by Gershen Kaufman and Lev Raphael.

Heroines and Heroes

Directions

Everyone has people they look up to. They can be athletes, performers, older brothers or sisters, teachers, or parents. These are our heroes and heroines.

Can you name three people you admire and want to be like? Write down their names. What is it about each one that you admire? Why? Write these things down too. What are some things you can do to be more like them? Are there any books or articles you can read about them? Do you have any photos or pictures? Keep a scrapbook or make a collage of your heroines and heroes.

Your notes and scrapbook will come in handy when you are planning your future and setting personal goals for yourself.

Richie Rich

Materials
Pencil
Paper
Calculator

Directions
You are going to pretend that a wealthy relative gave you $10,000. Her only stipulation is that you have to spend every penny on yourself. Imagine! You get to spend the entire amount on yourself. What will you do? Write down your spending plan in detail. Keep a tally of your spending using the calculator.

Share your plan with someone else. What comments and reaction did you receive? Did you learn something new about yourself now that you are rich? How did it feel to be told that you had to spend all the money on yourself?

Teach Yourself

Typing

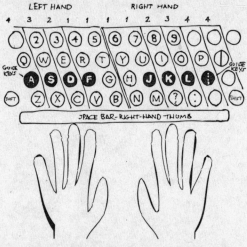

Material
Typewriter or computer

Directions
The most important thing to remember when learning to type is that it takes much practice! There are eight keys that are called "home keys." Your fingers must rest on these keys at all times except when a finger is moved to strike another key. Home keys are in black on the diagram. After striking the key, the finger must be returned immediately to its correct position. Practice by copying pages from books. Memorize the keys, then try not to look at them as you type. Study the diagram closely and notice the numbers at the top. They tell you which finger strikes each key. Keep practicing!

Note: There are many "teach yourself to type" books available in stores or at the library.

Perfume Making

Ingredients
Essential oils
Pure grain alcohol (vodka)
Water

Directions
Perfume is simple to make, the trick is to put the essential oils together creating a smell you like. Perfume is made up of base notes (the smell stays the longest on your skin), middle notes (smell stays second longest), and top notes (smell of oil evaporates first). Because the oils all evaporate at different rates the perfume may smell different as time goes on. Below are listed easily found essential oils divided into base, middle and top notes.

- Base notes—cedar wood, cinnamon, patchouli, sandalwood, vanilla
- Middle notes—clove, geranium, lemongrass, nutmeg, neroli, ylang-ylang
- Top notes—bergamot, lavender, lemon, lime, neroli
- Bridge—vanilla, lavender (add a few drops to join base, middle and top notes together)

To make your perfume, mix at least twenty-five drops total of essential oils divided evenly between base, middle, and top notes. Start with the base notes, then middle, then top, smelling as you go. Add a few drops of the bridge oil. Add two and a half ounces of alcohol (get a parent to help you with this), shake for a few minutes, then let it sit for forty-eight hours (or up to six weeks—the longer it sits, the stronger the smell). Add two tablespoons spring water, stir, then pour through a coffee filter and put in a bottle.

Sign Language

Directions

Sign language is a silent language done with the hands. Libraries have books on sign language. It is fun and easy to learn if you practice! Find a book with diagrams that are easily understood. Pick a poem or song you like and

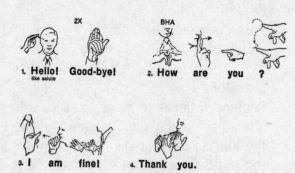

1. Hello! like salute Good-bye! 2. How are you ?

3. I am fine! 4. Thank you.

learn the words by looking them up in the book. The best way to learn sign language is to pick things you want to be able to say, then look the hand movements up in the book and practice them. It might be fun to learn with a friend so the two of you can talk silently together and nobody will know what you are saying. When you meet a deaf person you will be able to say something to them which will make both of you very happy!

Note: The illustrations are taken from the book *Sign Language Made Simple,* by Edgar D. Lawrence. This is an excellent book for beginners.

Tap Dancing

Materials
Metal taps bought at a dance supply store or metal bottle tops without the cork lining and short nails
Pair of shoes with hard soles

Directions
Fasten the metal taps following supplied directions or fasten the bottle tops with short nails, three of them in a triangular shape at the toe and two at the heel. Make sure the nails won't go through the sole of the shoe or the nails will cut your feet! Concrete, tiled, or wood floors make the best noises. Put the shoes on and experiment with different movements. Shake your body all over to get loosened up. Turn on some music you like and practice tapping your toe and heel with loose leg bones. Invent your own steps. If you want to learn more structured steps, get a book from the library or find a video on tap dancing. Classes are often available at your local community center or school.

Using a Sewing Machine

Materials
Sewing machine
Thread
Scraps of fabric

Directions
Sewing machines are easy to use, just be careful to keep your fingers away from the needle. It is important to ask

the person who owns the sewing machine to show you how to run that particular machine. Some questions to ask are:

1. How to turn it on
2. How to thread it
3. How the pedal works
4. How to guide the fabric to the needle

Once you know these things, take your scrap piece of fabric and practice. Make straight, curved, and zig-zag line patterns. To make a sharp turn, lift the machine foot leaving the needle in the fabric. Turn the fabric and set the foot down again. Once you have practiced enough, find a beginner pattern at a fabric store and follow the directions. You may need some help cutting the fabric out. There are sewing classes available at sewing machine stores.

Astronomy

Materials
Book on star constellations

Directions
Astronomy is the study of stars, planets, and other objects that make up the universe. Astronomers observe the sky and also ask questions like, "What are stars made of?" and "How do stars create light?" Some astronomers study through observation, viewing the sky through a  telescope. Go outside on a clear night and look at the stars. Read a little before you go out so you know what to look for. Try to find constellations like the Southern Cross, the Big Dipper, or others you see in the book. Go out different times of the year and do a little map of what you see. Does the sky change throughout the year?

World Hellos

Directions
Learning a foreign language is fun. People from all over the world live in the United States so you may be able to use your new words in your local community. Here is how to say "hello" around the world.

Bonjour—French
Hola—Spanish
Yassoo—Greek
Halloj—Danish
Zdrasvuytya—Russian
Shalom—Hebrew
Marhabah assalamu aleikum—Arabic
Ohayo gozaimasu—Japanese
G'Day—Australia
Haere-mai—Maori (New Zealand)

Learn About Business

Directions

A business can be anything that makes money. Making money is fun, and there are many ways to do it. A good way to learn about what adults do when they go to work is to ask them. Set up interviews with your parents and a few of their friends in the areas of interest to you. Ask them questions about the time they put in, how long it took to learn their craft, if they have to advertise, who works for them, who do they work for, how a product is manufactured, how products get into stores, if they take classes to learn about business, etc. You can also look in the library for books about business.

Yoga

Directions

Yoga is a form of exercise that teaches deep breathing and stretches. It is a way of relaxation, play, and better health. Once you learn the correct positions of the stretches and proper yoga breathing it is fun and easy to do. Try the morning exercise "Salute to the Sun" shown below. If you choose to try more yoga, there are many books and video tapes available.

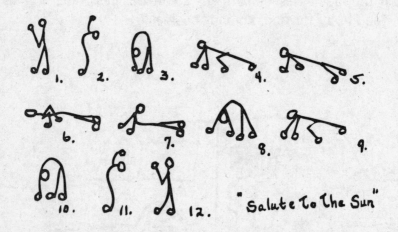

"Salute To The Sun"

Bird-Watching

Materials
Binoculars
Bird book for your area

Directions
Anywhere you go there will be birds. Get a book from the library to find out what kind of birds you can expect to see in your area. Birds owe their success as a species to their ability to fly. Flight enables birds to feed where other animals cannot, escape enemies, and move with the seasons. Birds in flight are a beautiful sight. Take your binoculars and look for birds flying and resting. A few things to look for when bird-watching:

- Type of bird
- Different beak shapes to cope with main food source—long or hooked beaks for tearing at prey, short and stout cone shapes to crack seeds.
- Feet—for different purposes like perching on twigs, running, clinging to trees, grasping prey, paddling in water.
- Color—to blend with environment or to stand out.
- Nests and eggs

Calligraphy

Materials
Calligraphy fountain pen
Left or right-handed nibs (pen points)
Ink cartridges
Ruled calligraphy practice pads

Directions
Calligraphy, or the art of "beautiful writing," originated with the Greek and Roman hand-lettered manuscripts. Take your calligraphy pen and practice the letters shown, following the arrow directions. If you like calligraphy, get a book that shows all sorts of letter shapes as well as giving directions to do them correctly. You can use your new skill to make Christmas cards, party invitations, poems to frame, personalized stationery, report covers, or story books.

ABCDEFGHI JKLMNOPQ RSTUVWX YZ0123456789

First Aid

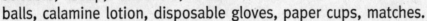

Materials

First aid kit: First aid information, bandages, gauze squares, adhesive tape, thermometer, ice pack, hydrogen peroxide, rubbing alcohol, syrup of ipecac, activated charcoal, scissors, soap, tweezers, cotton balls, calamine lotion, disposable gloves, paper cups, matches.

Directions

There is much to learn about first aid. Why not start by getting a first aid kit together for your family? Listed above are some basic supplies. There are first aid courses for kids. Call your community center, local hospital, or school to find out where they are. Listed bellow are a few basic things to know:

- Head injuries—if there is swelling, loss of consciousness, vomiting, change in the size of pupils of the eye, dizziness, or speech changes call 911.
- Broken bones—do not move unless in immediate danger, keep quiet and warm, do not try to straighten bone.
- Burns—with reddened to blistered skin immerse in cold water, if skin is destroyed call 911 and do not do anything to skin.
- Bleeding—to control, apply firm, steady pressure with covered fingers or hand over the wound itself and elevate.
- Choking, lack of breathing, and heart attacks are situations you can learn to deal with given correct information in a class.

Textiles

Stick Weaving

Materials
2 straight sticks equal in diameter and length
Yarn—three or four different colors
Scissors

Directions
Bind the two sticks together in a cross shape by holding them together in one hand and taking

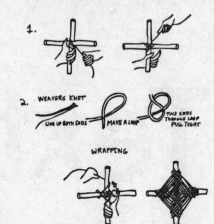

a long piece of yarn (thirty-six inches) in the other hand. Wrap the yarn tightly on a diagonal fifteen times in one direction then fifteen times in the other direction (see illustration 1). Once the sticks are tightly bound you may begin the weaving. You will have a loose end of yarn left after you wrap the diagonals, attach another piece of yarn of a different color by knotting the ends together (see illustration 2). The cross will be held in one hand, the weaving string in the other. Moving clockwise, wrap over and around the first stick (the closest to your weaving hand), then move clockwise to the next stick and again wrap the yarn over the top, then around clockwise to next stick. Continue, creating a diamond-shaped pattern. Knot on new colors of yarn as the old yarn is used up. Tie around stick when finished.

Hand Print Shirt

Materials
T-shirt (solid color or white)
Fabric or acrylic paint
Large piece of cardboard

Directions
Cut piece of cardboard so shirt can be stretched over it. This will prevent paint soaking through to the other side of the T-shirt. Put whatever paint color you want to use on a plate. Stick your hand in the paint then press your hand onto the shirt a couple of times until the hand print is faint. Do this as many times as you want with one color then switch to another color. Wash your hands and plate in between colors. If the shirt is a dark color, you may have to use acrylic paint so the color will show up. If you use fabric paint, go over the T-shirt with a medium hot iron when dry.

Note: You can also use feet for this project and print on rugs, aprons, or even a family wall hanging.

Shoelace Art

Materials
New white shoelaces
Fabric paint or markers
Puff paint

Directions
Decorate one side of each lace to your liking. Dry thoroughly, then decorate the other side. Do a few pairs so you can mix and match them in your shoes. These also make nice necklaces with large colored beads added. Think of other things you could do with them, like making lots of loops and gluing them to a hair clip, wrapping them around a plastic headband, gluing them around a pencil for a better grip, gluing them on anything as decoration. Keep thinking!

Yarn Dolls

Materials
Yarn or string
8-inch x 4-inch piece of cardboard
Scissors

Directions
Wind the yarn around the card about thirty times or until the yarn is about as fat as two fingers. Remove it from the card and tie a doubled wool strand around it and knot at the following locations:

- ½ inch down from top
- 1 inch down from that for the bottom of the head
- Take one bunch on each side and tie about 1 inch down for the arms
- 2½ inches down from head for waist
- Divide the remaining yarn and tie for legs
- Trim hair, hands, and feet

Make this doll some clothes out of fabric scraps and make a bed or room out of painted food boxes or give them as special gifts to friends.

Pillowcase Picture

Materials
Light colored pillowcase (new or used)
Fabric paint or markers
Large piece of cardboard

Directions
Decide what you want to paint on your pillowcase. Put the piece of cardboard inside where the pillow usually goes. It sometimes helps to have the fabric pulled tight over the cardboard, so you may have to do the painting in sections if the cardboard is small. Have fun painting your design. Let it dry, then have an adult iron over the finished pillowcase with a medium hot iron to set the paint. Wash before using.

Note: This is a great slumber party idea. Divide the pillowcase in sections and have each of your friends paint something on it and sign their name. It also makes a great moving away present for a friend.

Make a Sewing Kit

Materials
Felt and other fabric scraps
Needles
Thread
Buttons
Small scissors
Small tape measure
Yarn
Box
Glue

Directions
Sewing projects are much easier to begin if materials are in one place. Find a shoe box and cover the outside with scrap fabric glued to the outside of the box. Glue fabric inside the box and lid as well. Make a needle case out of felt to keep your needles together. Cut a square, then cut a long rectangle one inch wider and three and a half times longer than the square. Pin the square in the middle and straight stitch around the square. Put the needles into the smaller square and fold the ends over the top. This keeps your fingers from being pricked when you select a needle. Ask people for scraps of fabric, old buttons, thread, thimbles, yarn, small containers to store buttons and pins, or anything you think you might need.

Appliqué

Materials
Fabric for background
Felt or other fabric
Needle
Thread and yarn
Straight pins
Fabric marker

Directions
Sewing fabric shapes on top of another piece of fabric is called appliqué. Many times the shape sewn on has a little padding stuffed inside to make it stand out. It is fun to decorate these shapes with stitching using different colors of yarn as you might use markers to color a picture. First decide on the shape of the appliqué. You may want to draw it on cardboard, cut it out and place it on the felt, then outline with a fabric marker. If you make templates out of cardboard you can use them again. Pin your shape onto the background fabric and sew on the shape with small straight stitches. Stuff a little padding in before you finish sewing it on if you want it to stick up. Decorate with different kinds of stitches.

Embroidery

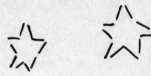

Materials

Threads and yarn of different sizes
and textures
Needles—assorted sizes to match
yarn and thread
Light colored fabric
Embroidery ring

Directions

Embroidery is making patterns with
stitches. You can make marks on fabric
with thread just as you can with a pen-
cil on paper. Put the fabric in the embroidery ring to hold it taut. Decide
on a design and pencil it onto the fabric. Thread one of the needles with
a length of yarn about twelve inches and knot the end. Use a straight
stitch, which is simply putting the needle under the ring and coming up
through the fabric. Make the length of stitch you want and go back
down through the fabric. This simple straight stitch can make all sorts
of patterns. By using different sizes and textures of yarn you can create
interesting effects.

Pocket Wall Hanging

Materials
Felt
Scissors
Needle and thread
Stick pins

Directions
Cut out a rectangle the size you want your wall hanging to be. Decide on pocket size. Cut pockets out of felt. Pin them where you want them on the large rectangle. Sew around the edges leaving the top of each pocket open. Sew a piece of yarn across the back to hang or tack to the wall. Fill pockets with miniature toys, figures, art supplies, letters, trading cards, etc.

Woven Ring

Materials
1 wooden ring 8-inches to 12-inches wide
1 sharp needle
1 tapestry needle
Large beads
Yarn—9-inches to 12-inches long strong pieces in a variety of textures

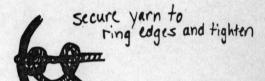

secure yarn to ring edges and tighten

Directions
Knot eight of the yarn pieces across the ring spaced evenly and tied as shown. To add beads, tie one end to the outside edge of the ring then add the bead and tie the other end. Knot the ninth piece of string to the ring edge, then take the other end to the middle and knot around all the other yarns. After they are tied properly around the edge cut the end leaving a half inch. Cover the rest of the ring by wrapping yarn around, trapping and securing the knots along the ring as you go. To make weaving easier, make a shuttle as shown and wrap the yarn around it. When you finish the yarn on the shuttle, secure the end by threading it through a sharp needle and push it back through the weaving. Start a new yarn the same way. Weave with different textures and colors.

Visual Arts

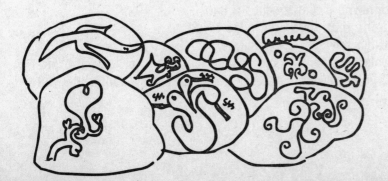

Shapes to See

Materials
Large piece of paper
Markers

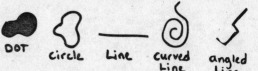

Directions
Everything you will ever want to draw is made out of five simple shapes, the circle (anything roundish that is empty), the dot (anything roundish that is colored in), the straight line, the curved line, and the angled line (see illustration). Do an abstract drawing (that means it doesn't look like any recognizable form) using the different shapes. Follow these directions:

1. Using two different colored felt tip pens, make four straight lines from one edge of the paper to the other. The lines can cross if you like.
2. Create three dots on your paper any size or shape.
3. Starting at one of the dots, make a curved line that goes off the page.
4. Make a circle somewhere that touches a line.
5. Make an angled line that goes from edge to edge.
6. Color in your design however you want.
7. As you take a walk outside, or look around your room, or look at a picture book, see if you can identify these shapes and think about how you would draw what you see!

Still Life Drawing

Materials
Paper
Pencil, markers, or crayons

Directions
To draw your still life, you will need to learn
how to overlap. Overlapping is simply drawing objects in front of each other. This makes your drawing look more interesting and real. Overlapping is easy if you remember the following rules:
1. Draw the object that is in front first.
2. Draw the object that is behind next, and when you run into something, stop, jump over it, and keep going on the other side with the same line.

First try this using shapes like circles, squares, ovals, rectangles (see example). Now set up your "still life" (still life means an arrangement of non-moving objects). Some good objects are tea pots, cups, vases, bowls, fruit, flowers, stuffed animals, or anything else you can find. Set them up in a group in front of you making sure some are in front of others. Now using the concept of overlapping, draw the object in front first, then continue.

Note: An excellent resource on learning to draw is the book *Drawing with Children,* by Mona Brooks.

Look and Draw

Materials
Paper
Pencil, markers, or crayons
Picture from a book or magazine
you want to draw

Directions
Artists look at existing images in
real life, pictures, and other artwork in order to draw. They look
at these things to copy shape
and form, then they use their own imagination to take things out or add
things, ending up with a completely original work of art. Drawing skills
are learned through imitation. When you pick something to draw, make
sure it is something you like. To start, take a scrap piece of paper and
make a warm-up drawing. Look at the object, put your pencil on the
paper, and without looking at the paper or taking the pencil off the
paper, draw the object. As you move on to the "good" paper, remember to look for the five shapes (activity 334) and do the drawing one
shape at a time!

Drawing Faces

Materials
Paper and pencil
Ruler
Mirror

Directions
Did you know that your eyes are in the middle of your head? Look closely at a mirror and bring your ruler to do some measuring.

- The face is two-thirds as wide as it is tall.
- The eyes are about halfway up the face.
- The distance from the eyebrows to the base of the nose is the same as the distance from the base of the nose to the tip of the chin.
- The space between the eyes equals one eye length.

These measurements vary slightly from person to person (small babies and young children have a little different proportion). Measure your face by looking closely and taking a few notes. Go away from the mirror and draw a self-portrait (a picture of your face). A self-portrait will not look exactly like you, but it will give some basic information that might make it resemble you. Keep practicing!

Window Picture

Materials
2 large pieces of paper (the same size)
Markers, crayons, felt tip pens, or paint
Scissors, glue, ruler

Directions
Draw or paint a picture of an outside scene like a lake with boats on it, a garden, a house or building, or anything you like. It is best to go outside and draw as you look at a scene. When the picture is done, cut a window frame out of the other piece of paper. Glue it over the top of your picture to make it look like the view from a window.

Story Mobile

Materials
Crayons, felt tip pens, colored pencils, or paint
9 x 24-inch strip of thick, light colored paper or poster board
String, scissors, stapler

Directions
Decide on a story you would like your pictures to tell. Take the strip of paper or poster board and evenly divide it into the number of pictures you plan to draw. Color in the entire strip so the design isn't lost when light shines through. When drawings are completed, bend the strip around into a large cylinder. Staple it at the top and bottom. Take three pieces of string of equal length and attach them to the top of the cylinder in three evenly spaced spots. Carefully use the tip of the scissors to make tiny holes. Tie the string to the picture strip, then tie all three strings together at the top. You could also try gluing favorite photographs onto the strip creating a "photo mobile."

Design a Stamp

Materials
Piece of white paper
Crayons or markers
Scissors, pencil

Directions
Think of a picture dealing with your country, holidays, people, sport, or a special event that you think would look good on a stamp. Sketch your idea lightly in pencil on the paper. Choose one of the following ways to color the stamp.

- Choose one color of crayon and complete the drawing using different tones of that color.
- Use a variety of colors.

Write the price of the stamp somewhere within the composition. When the coloring is done, cut around the edges of the stamp in either points or scallops.

Note: It is fun to collect stamps as they come in the mail and get some ideas.

Optical Illusion

Materials
Paintbrush
Paint
Scissors
9 x 12-inch paper
9 x 24-inch heavy paper (can be taped together)
Hair spray or clear acrylic

Directions
Make two paintings that are very different from each other. It is good to make them basic, with large objects in them like a child's picture book. Opposite ideas like winter and summer, day and night, or land and sea, work well. When the paintings are dry, turn them over and make marks one inch apart along the top and bottom. Connect the marks with lines to make strips. Number the strips one to twelve from left to right. Cut the strips apart and glue them onto the large paper. Glue number one from the first painting from right to left, then number one from the other painting and so on until all twelve strips from each painting are glued on in order. Fold the paper like an accordion, one fold for each strip. Spray with hair spray or acrylic. Look at your painting from one direction and you will see one painting, look from the other direction and you will see the other painting.

Fold and Dip Designs

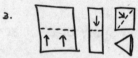

Materials
Vegetable food colors
Muffin pans
Paper towels, tissue paper,
rice paper, or watercolor paper
Newspaper to cover work area

Directions
First, cover the work area with newspaper,
then fill the pans with a mixture of water and food color. Have at least
six colors. Red + blue = purple; yellow + red = orange; blue + yellow =
green. The more color used, the darker the dye color. To start, fold the
paper in one of the following ways:

1. Pleat the paper back and forth like a fan, then fold the entire pleat in
   half and dip the corners, ends, and sides into the dye. Open up and lie
   flat on the newspaper to dry.
2. Make pleated fan as above, but this time pleat the entire shape into a
   small version of a fan. Dip each corner and lie flat to dry.
3. Fold the paper in half two times. Fold one corner to the other corner to
   form a triangle. Dip each corner, then carefully bend back corners and dip
   the middle section. Open, lie flat and dry.

Sand Painting

Try experimenting with your own folds. Use dyed paper for wrapping or stationery.

Materials

Colored sand from a craft store
Glue, pencil
Sandpaper
Cookie sheet
Paint brush
Book on Indian designs (optional)

Directions

Draw a design on the sandpaper with a pencil. Put the colored sand in separate dishes. Put one tablespoon glue and one tablespoon water into a bowl. Put the sandpaper on the cookie sheet. Start with the lightest color of sand and decide all the places you want that color on the painting, then brush the glue onto those places. Now use a spoon to sprinkle the lightest color of sand onto the glued sections. Turn the sandpaper over and the loose sand will fall back into the cookie sheet. Let dry for ten minutes. Pour the leftover sand back into its original dish. Do the same for each color of sand. Let dry thoroughly.

Rock Painting

Materials
Large or small rocks and stones
Acrylic paint
Paint brush

Directions
When you collect the stones, look
for ones with interesting shapes
that might add to the design.
Wash and dry your rock. Decide on what you will paint. Use dots, circles, squares, and stripes to add interest. When the paint is dry, you
may want to cover it with a clear varnish. Painted rocks make great
gifts. Here are a few ideas: paperweights, small stones as friendship
gifts, a purse pal for mom, decoration for the garden, doorstop, or
bookend. You can even glue rocks together using a strong bonding
cement.

Melted Crayon Painting

Materials
Cookie sheet or warming tray
Foil
Paper
Fat wax crayons

Directions
Cover the cookie sheet with foil and place in the oven at 250°F (130°C) for ten minutes. Or if you have a warming tray, plug it in and set it on low. Peel the paper off the crayons while the tray or cookie sheet is heating. Place

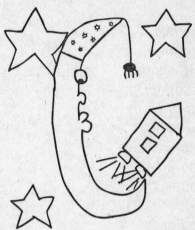

your paper on the warm surface and draw slowly so the crayon has a chance to melt. Use the side of the crayon to paint fat lines. Use an old comb to make interesting lines. Be careful not to touch the tray and burn yourself. Once the painting is cool, cut shapes out and glue them onto another piece of paper as a collage. Or paint the picture directly onto the foil, then put a piece of white paper on top and make a print.

Note: In ancient Greece, artists used to paint with wax. This was called encaustic painting.

Puff Paint

Materials
Paintbrush
Food coloring
Scissors
Glue
Squeeze bottles
1 cup water
1 cup flour
1 cup salt

Directions
Make puff paint to outline and accent a painting. Mix the water, flour, and salt and divide it into several dishes. Add food coloring to make a different color in each dish. Fill each bottle with a different color, or if you have only one bottle, squeeze one color in all the places you want that color to be. Wash the bottle and use it for the other colors.

Note: You can make many fun things with puff paint, like picture frames, decorative boxes, light switch covers, or special cards.

Watercolor Glue Painting

Materials
White glue
Black acrylic paint
Paper
Watercolors
Paintbrush
Old glue bottle or plastic bags

Directions
Make a pencil drawing on paper.
Mix one teaspoon of black acrylic
paint with three teaspoons of white glue and stir. If you have an old
squeeze glue container, put the glue in that. If not, put the glue in a
plastic bag, then make a tiny cut in the corner. Squeeze the glue along
the pencil lines. Let the glue dry and then take watercolor paints and
paint the rest of the picture. Felt tip pens will also work to color in the
drawing if you want very bright, strong colors.

Scratch Pictures

Materials
White cardboard
Black India ink
Wax crayons
Black poster paint
Paintbrush
Sharp tool to scratch with (broken pencil or piece of sharp wood)

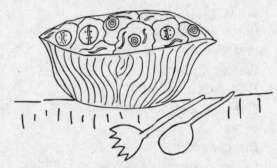

Directions
Cover the white card with thick and vivid layers of wax crayon. Paint over the design with a mixture of half black poster paint and half India ink. When the paint is dry, use a sharp tool to scratch a picture or design into the paint. As you scratch, you will reveal the wax colored design underneath.

Q-Tip Painting

Materials
Q-Tips
Light colored paper
Paint
Scratch paper
Muffin tin

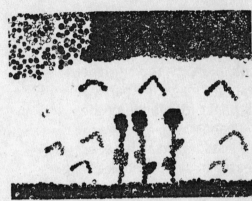

Directions
You may want to do a rough sketch of your design on scratch paper before starting. Pour paints into tins, dip the Q-Tip into the paint, and fill in your sketch with paint dots. This type of painting works well on small pieces of paper and is good for greeting cards, a small square on a report cover, or within a larger picture as a picture on the wall. Be careful not to smudge the dots with your hand. You may want to let each color dry before adding a new color. This can be done quickly using a hair dryer.

Torn Paper Pictures

Materials
Paper—construction paper of different colors, wrapping paper, newsprint, magazine paper
Dark paper for mounting the torn shapes
Glue, scissors, scratch paper
Resource material—books, magazines, album covers, etc.

Directions
Put the large piece of dark paper on a tabletop. Decide if you would like to do an abstract design of shapes (which means it won't be recognizable), or a realistic design (which looks like something specific such as a person, place, or thing). If you decide to do a realistic design, you may want to look at a picture in a book so you can easily re-create the shapes you see. Do a rough sketch on the scratch paper just to get an idea of layout. Now start tearing paper into various shapes. The rough uneven edges add personality. Glue the torn pieces onto the dark paper creating the desired picture.

Writing

The Me Book

Materials
Paper
Pen or pencil
Crayons, felt tips, or paint
Pictures of the family

Directions
An autobiography is the story of a person's life, and who knows more about your life than you! This is going to be a book about you, the people, the places, the events, your interests, feelings, and dreams. A good place to begin is with your first memories, then you could write your story in the order that your life happened up until today. Another way is to have chapters and each chapter describes one aspect of your life. The chapters could be things like: my family, my friends, school, my dreams, funny moments, what my parents say, when I grow up. The topics are endless. Give yourself some time to write it. The end result will be a treasure to you when you're older!

Binding a Book

Materials
Paper
String
Large-eyed needle

Directions
A hand sewn book is easier to read because the pages lie flat. It also lasts longer. First, decide on the size of your book. You

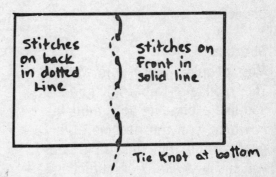

Stitches on back in dotted line

stitches on Front in solid line

Tie Knot at bottom

will be folding the paper in half and sewing up the middle, so the paper needs to be twice as long as you want each page to be. Open the book and make a pencil dot every few inches in a straight line down the middle of the paper. Take a ruler and measure the line, then place a dot every one to two inches so your stitching will be even. Thread enough string so you have three times the line's length. Start at the bottom, leaving four inches of thread for tying a knot when you are finished. Now push the needle through the paper (see illustration). Go up the book following the darker line, first one big stitch on one side, then one big stitch on the other side. Once you reach the top, go back down following the lighter line.

Notebook

Materials
Blank notebook

Directions
Most people are not born writers. They work at it to become good. If you like expressing your thoughts in words, you can become a very good writer by practicing. Get yourself a notebook or journal and write in it 15 minutes every day. Write anything you want—write about your feelings, describe your day, write a story, describe a person you meet, write words you like, write anything, just WRITE!

Beginnings

Directions

Sometimes it is hard to begin a story. Your story could begin with dialogue (people talking to each other), a narrator's summary (of an event that has happened), or a description (of a character, place, or event). The most important thing is that the "beginning" must  begin in the middle of things. Resist the urge to write all the details about how things got to this point. The details can be added as the story progresses. You may not even know where the story is going or how it will end. To practice beginnings, write five opening lines for five different stories. Here are a few examples:

- Returning from the mailbox Brooke searched through the pile of letters.
- Mysterious things happen in that blue house on the hill.
- "I really like you," Wesley said as she walked toward the front door.
- Looking around the room you could see Rhett had talent.
- "Where were you last night?" Mom asked.

Characters

Directions

Characters are the living beings in your story, the ones that talk and interact with people. When you meet someone in real life, you notice things about them like their age, clothes, haircut, type of accent, if they smile, and many others. As a writer, you must supply your readers with all sorts of written clues that paint a picture

of your character. You must describe in words how your character acts each day, what she is afraid of, who her friends are, and what she likes to do. The fun part is that you make it all up. There are no rules, your characters come from your imagination. Your stories may contain many different characters, for example, an old man, a small baby, or a school bully. You have to write about them without having ever been in their life. That is why observation (watching people to see how they do things) is so important. Think of a character, then write a description about him or her. Write as many things as you can create. Do this a few times with different kinds of people, old, young, male, female, teacher, mother, baby, etc. When you are done writing, give your character a name! You may want to keep these in your notebook and use them in stories.

Dialogue

Directions

Dialogue is two or more characters talking to each other. What the characters say to each other needs to move the story along. You can do this by having one character tell another what's happening, reveal a plan, admit to some-thing they did, or accuse somebody of doing something. Dialogue also tells us about the person. For example, a mother would use different words than a five-year-old boy, an angry principal will sound different than a circus clown. Try writing a dialogue between two friends that disagree about something, or a mother and daughter, or an old gardener and a young child. Remember, it is practice that makes a good writer.

Note: Be like a detective and listen to how people say things in your everyday life, then use their words in your story dialogues.

Plot

Directions

A story has a beginning, a middle, and an end. Everything that happens in the story depends on the character. You place a character in a situation and then discover what happens. The plot is really what a character decides to do, usually with some difficulty.

Take Cinderella for example:
1. Cinderella can't go to the ball (beginning)
2. She goes anyway (middle)
3. Cinderella gets prince (end)
- Make up a character, then think of a situation to put them in.
- What does the character do in that situation?
- What happens when they do this?

Write these three sentences down as above in Cinderella. That will be your basic story plot. Now all you have to do is add descriptions of characters and dialogue!

Storytelling

Directions

Tell a story today. Retell a story you have read, heard, or seen, or make one up in your imagination. Write down a few sentences to describe the beginning, middle, and end. The challenge is to give enough description of characters, scene, and action to give your audience a mental picture. You may want to practice your words and facial expressions in front of a mirror before you tell the story to an audience. This is a fun way to test stories you make up to see if you like them enough to write down.

Read It, Write It

Materials
Favorite books

Directions
Think about the reasons you like your favorite book. Did you like the character? Did you feel you knew the character by the end? Did you like the way the author wrote? Did you like the story? Copying the writing style of an

author you like is a good way to learn. Open the book to the first page, go halfway down the first paragraph and insert a sentence you make up to go between sentences the author has written. Try to make it sound similar in style to the author's sentence. Do this in a few places throughout the book.

Note: Whenever you read a book, write down sentences you like in your notebook. Notice the words that are used. To increase your vocabulary, write down words you don't know, look them up in the dictionary, then use them in your next story.

Half Book

Materials

9 x 12-inch construction paper or poster board
9 x 6-inch construction paper or poster board
9 x 6-inch writing paper
Markers, crayons, pen or pencil
Scissors, stapler

Finished

Front Cover

Back cover

Out At Sea

My Frog

Directions

Half books work if you write a story that has one main character or theme. You draw a picture on the 9 x 12-inch poster board that in some way relates to each page. The large picture is the back cover. For the front cover, repeat the bottom half of the illustration on the 9 x 6-inch poster board. The story is written on the 9 x 6-inch writing paper. Staple the front cover and the story pages to the back cover. Write the title and the author's name on the front.

Book in a Bag

Materials
Paper lunch bag
3 x 5-inch writing paper
Construction paper scraps
Crayons, markers
Scissors, stapler, glue

Directions
A paper bag book has a character glued to the upper flap and a story stapled below. Here's how to make it. Write a story on the 3 x 5-inch writing paper. Put the bag on a table with the bottom of the bag flap toward you. Fold the top of the bag under the flap. Open the bag and staple the completed story pages below the fold line. Draw and cut out a character from the story and glue it to the flap of the bag. Make arms, wings, tail, or any other accents out of construction paper and glue to the side of the bag to add character. Fold up the bottom half containing the story and tuck under the flap. Write the title of the book and the author's name.

Note: Use this for a book report, holding it like a puppet in front of the class.

Letter Book

Materials
Cardboard or cardstock
10 to 12 envelopes
Paper
Pen and felt tips

Directions
A letter book consists of separate letters that each tell a little story. The letters are all on a similar theme, for example: letters from the boys in Neverland, mail from around the world, pet mail, letters to friends, Dear Mr. President, my Olympic journey. The list could be endless. To begin, cut the flaps off all the envelopes. You design each piece of stationery, then write the letter. Fold the letter and put it inside the envelope. Address the envelope. Design a stamp and make a postmark. Make front and back cover out of the cardstock. Staple at the edge or take your book to a copy shop to be spiral bound.

Travelogue

Materials

4 x 20-inch strip of paper
(can be glued together)
2 sheets of 9 x 12-inch
construction paper
4 x 10-inch writing paper
Scissors, stapler, glue
Crayons or markers

Directions

Decorate the top half of one sheet of the 9 x 12-inch construction paper leaving the middle section plain (see illustration). Cut along lines A and B so the strip of pictures can slide through. Write about a vacation you have had or a place you want to travel to. For every page of story, draw a picture on the strip of paper making sure the picture fits inside the space between lines A and B. Make a cover and staple it to the front, then write the title and author's name on it. This can be used for other kinds of stories also. What else can you think of?

Invisible Ink

Materials
Lemon
Bowl
Q-Tips or pen that is out of ink
Paper
Iron

Directions
Here is your chance to write secret messages to friends! Cut the lemon in half and squeeze both halves into a bowl. Dip the Q-Tip or pen into the lemon juice and then write a message on a piece of paper. The message will show up when the paper is pressed with a very hot iron (a job done by someone who knows how to work the iron).

364

Accordion Card

Materials
12 x 36-inch (approximate)
butcher paper
2 pieces of cardboard
Colored pens, paints, crayons, or
markers
Scissors
Writing paper
Glue

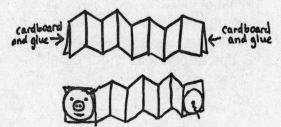

Directions
Fold the butcher paper in half lengthwise, then fold the butcher paper
accordion style into equal parts. The size of the resulting sections will
determine what size cardboard and writing paper you use. Glue a piece
of cardboard inside the front and back section and glue the bottom
edges. Make a front and back cover out of construction paper and glue
it on. Here are some ideas of what to write inside your card: why I love
you, all about me, what I did on my summer vacation, important activities I do each day, what to do when you're sad, the new baby. Send
the card to someone special!

About the Authors

Sheila Ellison is the author of nine books; founder of the nonprofit organization, Single Moms Connect; creator of an online mothering community www.CompleteMom.com; and a mother of four and stepmother of two. She has appeared on *Oprah!*, and her work has been featured in *O: The Oprah Magazine*, *Parenting*, *Family Circle*, *Ladies Home Journal*, *Glamour*, *Self*, the *New York Daily News*, the *San Francisco Chronicle*, and the *Oakland Tribune*.

Dr. Judith Gray is internationally known as an author, teacher, leader in dance research, and speaker on future trends in education and dance. A former Executive Director of the Girl's Club of Tucson, Dr. Gray has been an educator at both the high school and university level. A mother of four, she is currently helping to develop a state-of-the-art high school in the Everett School District, Washington, and is on the Antioch University teaching faculty. Dr. Gray is also the co-author of *365 Foods Kids Love to Eat*.

Notes

_____

_____

_____

_____

_____

_____

_____

_____

_____

_____

_____

Notes

Notes

Notes

_____

_____

_____

_____

_____

_____

_____

_____

_____

_____

_____

Notes

_____

_____

_____

_____

_____

_____

_____

_____

_____

_____

_____

_____

Notes

Notes

_____

_____

_____

_____

_____

_____

_____

_____

_____

_____

_____

_____